D0649625

To the Cloud:

CLOUD POWERING AN ENTERPRISE

Pankaj Arora
Raj Biyani
Salil Dave

New York Chicago San Francisco Lisbon
London Madrid Mexico City Milan New Delhi
San Juan Seoul Singapore Sydney Toronto

The McGraw-Hill Companies

Cataloging-in-Publication Data is on file with the Library of Congress

McGraw-Hill books are available at special quantity discounts to use as premiums and sales promotions, or for use in corporate training programs. To contact a representative, please e-mail us at bulksales@mcgraw-hill.com.

To the Cloud: Cloud Powering an Enterprise

1 2 3 4 5 6 7 8 9 0 DOC DOC 1 0 9 8 7 6 5 4 3 2 1

ISBN 978-0-07-179221-9
MHID 0-07-179221-X

Sponsoring Editor
Wendy Rinaldi

Editorial Supervisor
Patty Mon

Project Manager
Harleen Chopra, Cenveo Publisher Services

Acquisitions Coordinator
Ryan Willard

Copy Editor
Lisa Theobald

Proofreader
Lisa McCoy

Indexer
Jack Lewis

Production Supervisor
George Anderson

Composition
Cenveo Publisher Services

Illustration
Cenveo Publisher Services

Art Director, Cover
Jeff Weeks

Contents

Foreword

I have yet to hear a business partner complain that "IT is moving much too fast—I wish they'd slow down a little," or that "I can't think of anything else I want IT to do to enable my business—they've covered all the bases already." Instead, we in IT are often viewed as the bottleneck, the naysayers, or the laggards.

Cloud computing can change that.

Although it can help reduce operating costs, I think the real promise of the cloud lies in its ability to help us fashion what I call the "real-time enterprise"—one that demands faster application development, a constant stream of data, and a responsiveness to business needs that just isn't achievable with planning and refresh cycles that are years long.

To me, the question isn't whether cloud computing is coming. The question is, now that the era of cloud computing has arrived, how soon will enterprise IT get on board?

For CIOs, cloud computing evokes a range of emotions—from hope and excitement to skepticism and fear. The overall response I hear is that cloud computing technology needs time to mature. Some think it will be ready to use in 18 months. Others estimate it will be five years before they will move. Concerns fall into several broad categories:

- **Economics** The current economic climate is encouraging IT departments to evaluate cloud computing as a path to cost reduction. Nearly everyone assumes cloud computing will be a cheaper alternative to on-premises models, but many question the ability to calculate the return on investment (ROI) and the long-term savings. ROI, for example, will be a function of many things, including the size, maturity, and complexity of an organization.
- **Complexity** Adopting cloud computing is not an all-or-nothing proposition. Most organizations will find that a hybrid environment with some on-premises and some cloud elements will best meet their needs. For CIOs, the question then becomes how to manage the complexity of this hybrid IT environment.
- **Security** CIOs puzzle over how they will assure their organization, customers, and partners that information stored in or passed through the cloud is safe. They also worry about protecting sensitive corporate data if the information isn't on-premises.

- **Performance** CIOs worry that moving to the cloud will mean trading one set of performance headaches for another. They wonder whether off-premises services will be as reliable as on-premises services. They're concerned about outages, bandwidth limitations, and insufficient service levels.

At Microsoft, we've been asking the same questions, and we're finding answers as we develop products for the cloud and test them in-house. Like many enterprise IT organizations, we pride ourselves on being early adopters of emerging technologies. For that reason, our IT team takes its role as "Microsoft's first and best customer" very seriously.

- In 2010, we successfully migrated components of our corporate website, Microsoft.com, to Windows Azure. At the time of writing, we're in the process of re-engineering two very visible Microsoft applications: our software-licensing platform and our employee performance evaluation application.
- The licensing platform is arguably our most critical application ecosystem—and one of our oldest. This collection of tools processes billions of dollars of revenue each quarter. Spikes in activity at the close of each month, quarter, and year made this legacy system an excellent candidate for moving to an elastic cloud-based solution.
- The performance evaluation application gets used by every Microsoft employee twice a year and is pretty much idle the rest of the time. It, too, presents a great opportunity for us to take advantage of the cloud's scale-out, scale-down capacity.

We're currently evaluating all applications we use for cloud opportunities, and based on our experience so far, our goal is to build all new IT applications in the cloud.

That's why I think this book is worth reading. It is written for CIOs and IT professionals, from the perspective of a CIO. It is informed by the questions we repeatedly hear and the best practices we've established during our own cloud journey. I think you'll find it thought-provoking and informative, and I hope it will encourage you to be as excited about the possibilities of the cloud as I am.

Tony

Tony Scott
Chief Information Officer
Microsoft Corporation
Redmond, Washington
January 2012

Acknowledgments

This book would not have been possible without the gracious support of many individuals. The personal guidance, vision, and encouragement of Microsoft CIO, Tony Scott, set the stage for this idea to turn into reality. For their leadership and encouragement, we also thank Jim DuBois, Vice President of Microsoft IT Engineering, and Shahla Aly, Vice President of IT Solutions Delivery. For his highly insightful and constructive feedback, we thank Barry Briggs, Microsoft IT CTO.

S. Somasegar, Corporate Vice President of the Developer Division at Microsoft, provided tremendous support and coaching, including insightful tips on the companion website for this book. We are grateful for the sponsorship from Satya Nadella, President, and Robert Wahbe, Corporate Vice President of Marketing, in the Server & Tools Division at Microsoft.

Bhaskar Pramanik, Chairman of Microsoft-India, inspired us to think about the immense potential of the cloud in emerging markets, such as Brazil, China, and India. These conversations resulted in the Epilogue, "Emerging Markets and the Cloud."

The writing of this book has been a collaborative effort. We sincerely appreciate the assistance, input, and feedback given by our colleagues across Microsoft:

Alain Crozier, Alan Stone, Amit Chatterjee, Amit Sircar, Amitabh Srivastava, Anand Krishnan, Ashish Soni, Bart Robertson, Beverly Carey, Bill Koefoed, Bill Laing, BJ Moore, Bob Anderson, Brad Sutton, Bret Arsenault, Chris Kuhl, Chris Pirie, Chris Sinco, Dave Gasiewicz, David Lef, Dee Dee Walsh, Donna Conner, Erin Dickerson, Frank Holland, Gina Dyer, Gretchen Oldberg, Ian Hill, Jacky Wright, Janakiram MSV, Jean-Philippe Courtois, Jeff Allen, Jeff Finan, John Williams, Jon Roskill, Justin Nelson, Kristy Bride, Kuleen Bharadwaj, Kurt Beard, Lakshmi Sulakshana, Lynn Kepl, Manuvir Das, Mark Wright, Matt Hempey, Matt Kellerhals, Meenu Handa, Michael Kogeler, Michael Yamartino, Mike Olsson, Neil Charney, Neil Holloway, Orlando Ayala, Patrick O'Rourke,

Price Oden, Rakesh Kumar, Rolf Harms, Sanket Akerkar, Sean Nolan, Srini Koppolu, Steve Levin, Susan Hauser, Tanuj Vohra, Tarlochan Cheema, Tim Sinclair, Tony Oliver, Trupti Deo, Venkat Bhamidipati, Vijay Vashee, Vikram Bhambri, Walter Puschner, and Yen-Ming Chen

We would like to thank our colleague and long-time Microsoft veteran, Nadine Kano, for her editorial and writing contributions.

We would like to thank Kris Gopalakrishnan, Executive Co-Chairman of Infosys Limited, for providing the Cloudvolution case study. We thank Sanjai Verma for providing the Government of India Income Tax Central Processing Center e-governance case study. We also thank Phanindra Sama and Charan Padmaraju for providing the redBus case study.

We would like to thank Wendy Rinaldi and all our partners at McGraw-Hill for their partnership in publishing, marketing, and distributing this book.

Since this book has been a labor of love that has consumed countless nights, weekends, and several holidays over the past year, we owe a ton of gratitude to our significant others for their sacrifice and support: Manisha Patel, Aarti Biyani, and Rashmi Dave.

Pankaj Arora Raj Biyani Salil Dave

Redmond, Washington
January 2012

Prologue

Business Value of IT

Today's enterprises, no matter what part of the world or what business they are in, strive to do three things simultaneously: sustain existing products and services, improve them, and introduce new ones. Gartner labels these three activities "run, grow, and transform." McKinsey uses the terms "stay in the race, win the race, and change the rules." This is what business is trying to do. What, in the meantime, has IT been doing?

IT has been supporting products and services. According to Gartner, in 2011, 66 percent of IT spending sustained existing products and services, 20 percent helped improve them, and 14 percent enabled the introduction of new products and services.[1] For the past six years, these percentages have barely changed year over year, even as globalization and competitive pressures have increased significantly. One would expect expenditures to move from "run" to "grow" and "transform," but that is not happening.

The numbers have stayed the same because transformational projects are transformational only as long as they provide a competitive advantage. No matter what technology you introduce into your enterprise environment, as long as it is relevant and adds value, more enterprises will adopt it as time goes on. Eventually, it will stop being a competitive advantage and will move to the "run" category. Twenty years ago, the first e-mail servers allowed companies to communicate faster with each other and with their customers, and this allowed them to get products to market faster. Today, every enterprise has e-mail. Thus, it has been in the "run" category for some time.

The time it takes IT to deliver new applications is also a factor. Businesses do not respond as quickly as market conditions change, and

[1]Source: Gartner, IT Metrics: Spending and Staffing Report, 2011, January 2011.

IT does not respond as quickly as business requirements change. If you plotted this phenomenon on a graph, it might look like the following illustration:

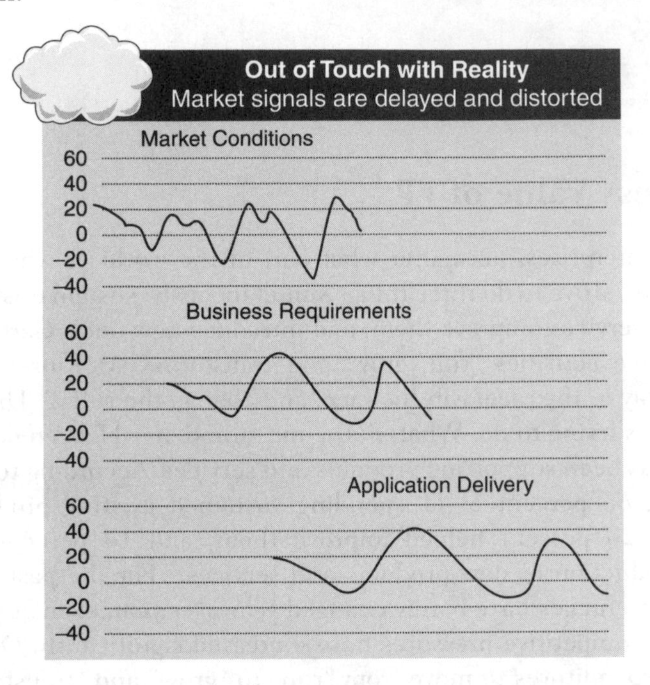

In fact, by the time IT delivers an application that meets a defined set of business requirements, market conditions might be completely different. The competitive advantage window might have passed, and the application, while brand new within the company, might only help "grow" or "run" the business. IT simply cannot keep up with "transform" opportunities.

Run, Grow, Transform

How does one measure the success of IT projects? IT projects whose missions do not go beyond helping the business "stay in the race" must reduce total cost of ownership (TCO). "Grow" projects, which improve existing products and services, must increase return on investment (ROI)—that is, help the business make more money. "Transform" projects that "change the game" must ultimately give the business a competitive advantage. Success depends on the business context, as shown in the following illustration:

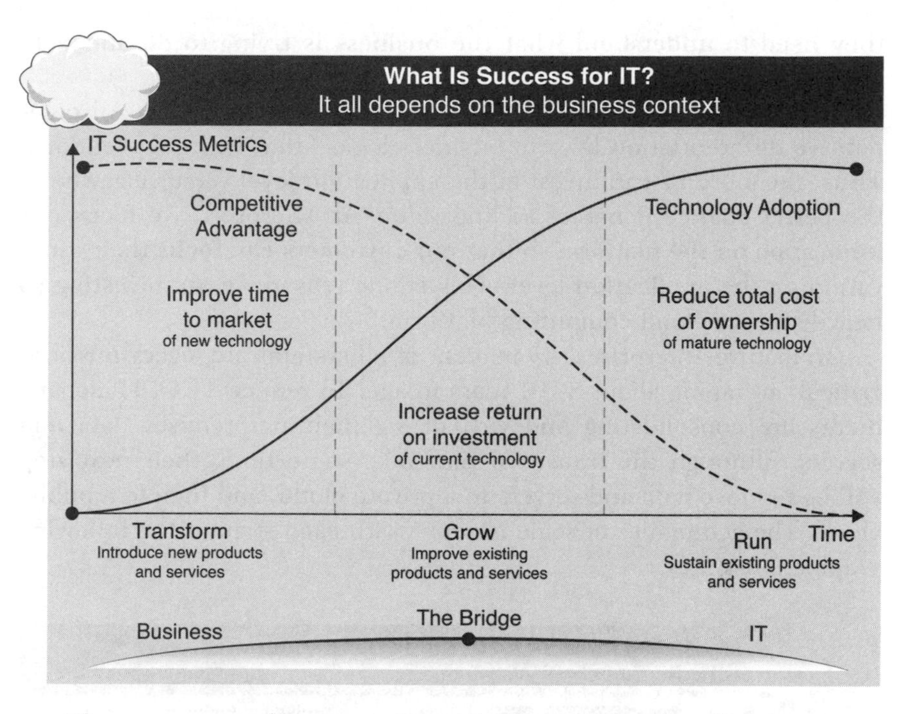

The spectrum of projects from "run" to "transform" presents an interesting challenge for IT. Business is most interested in the competitive advantage resulting from "transform" projects, but most IT focuses on reducing the TCO of "run" projects. Unfortunately, IT does not get a medal for reducing TCO. IT is *expected* to reduce TCO; IT gets to *keep its job* if it reduces TCO. IT gets a medal when its projects contribute to "grow" and "transform," which means IT must work closely with the business as a value-adding partner.

According to Deloitte's 2010 CIO survey, however, 60 percent of respondents did not think that business views IT as a value-adding partner, but rather saw IT as a cost center or supplier of services. At a company, to whom the CIO reports is a good indicator of the dynamics between business and IT. A 2010 Gartner survey showed that 38 percent of CIOs reported directly to the CEO; 19 percent reported to the COO (the supplier of services), and 25 percent reported to the CFO (the keeper of cost centers).[2] CIOs want a seat at the table—the CEO's table—but today most of them are not there. To get there, they need to be value-adding partners, and to be value-adding partners,

[2]Source: Gartner, Inc., CEO Advisory: When Should the CIO Report to the CEO?, January 2011. Data is from Gartner's EXP Global CIO Survey. Respondent numbers vary from 620 (2003) to 1,600 (2010).

they need to understand what the business is trying to do and help make that happen.

This is where IT's platform of choice becomes relevant. All competitive differentiation lives in business logic—that is, in applications. Thus, the more IT can invest at the application level versus elsewhere, the better chance it has of adding value. At Microsoft, we focus our innovation on the platform so that our customers can focus their innovation on the application level. This is one reason we are investing so heavily in our cloud computing platform.

In mature enterprises, 25 percent of all systems are legacy mission-critical, averaging about 8–10 years in age. To reduce TCO, IT departments are consolidating and virtualizing their on-premises data and servers. Although the transition may take some time, their next step will be to move data and servers to a private cloud, and then to a public cloud. The economies of scale improve with each step, as the following graphic illustrates.

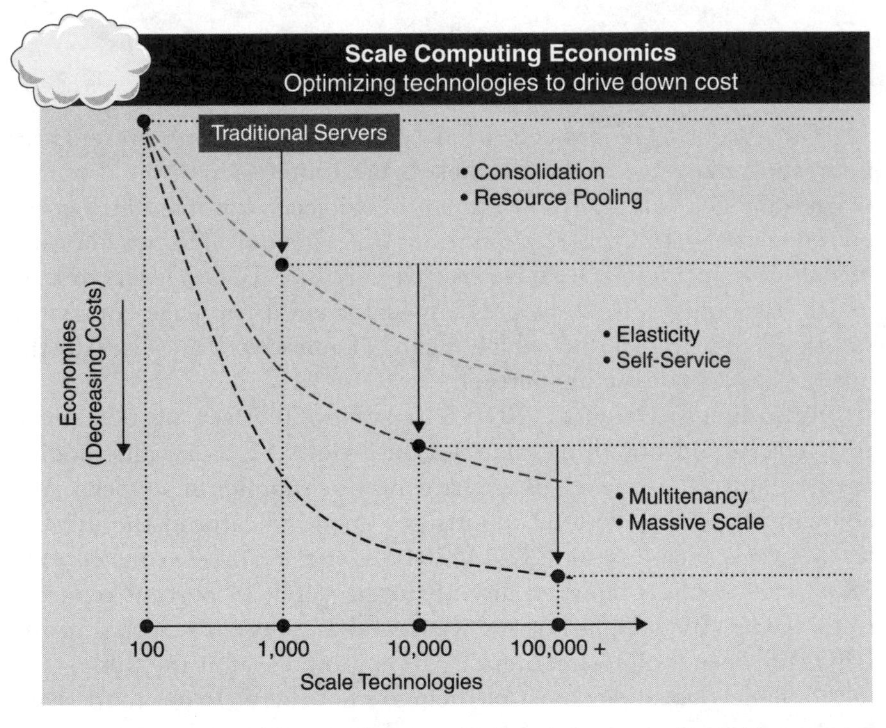

"Grow" projects are about improving productivity for users, developers, and IT professionals. Giving users and developers access to tools and services more quickly improves productivity, as does decreasing the time it takes to provision new infrastructure for running those tools and services. IT professionals and developers save time and effort because of the automated provisioning, scale-out, fault tolerance, and other features the cloud offers.

Most "transform" projects are bets, because it takes time before a business can quantitatively measure whether it will increase ROI or reduce TCO. Because you cannot always quantify what the actual benefit will be, the best course of action with a "transform" project is to make it operational as quickly as possible. The cloud lowers the expense and the risk of doing so. With resources that can be ready to go in minutes versus months, the cloud can give "transform" projects the agility to implement new business models quickly.

Cloud computing can reduce the burden on IT to manage "run" projects, offering more flexibility to accelerate "grow" and "transform" projects. It remains to be seen, but future surveys might find that companies that take advantage of the cloud shift more of their investment from "run" to the other categories. As that happens, IT's role can move from cost center or provider of services to value-adding partner for the business. This is one of the great promises of cloud computing.

Kuleen Bharadwaj
Group Product Manager, Server & Tools
Microsoft Corporation

tools and services. IT professionals and developers can [illegible] first [illegible] private [illegible] provisioning [illegible] tolerances and [illegible] directly [illegible] offices.

Most "transform" projects are bets, because it takes time before [illegible] quantitatively [illegible] whether it will increase ROI or reduce TCO. Because we cannot always quantify what the actual [illegible], the final choice of [illegible] make [illegible] as possible. [illegible] IT [illegible] changes [illegible]

[illegible] "transform" [illegible] that [illegible] to [illegible] and [illegible] IT [illegible] gain [illegible] to [illegible] help [illegible] competitive [illegible] compute [illegible]

[illegible]

[illegible] Manager, Server & [illegible]

[illegible] Microsoft Corporation

Introduction

From Mars to the Cloud

The sheer volume of information that rovers and orbiters send back from Mars is unmatched in the history of space exploration. U.S. National Aeronautics and Space Administration (NASA) databases store millions of detailed photographs, with new photos arriving every day.

For NASA, this huge influx of information coincided with another agency priority: finding ways to captivate the public with space exploration, particularly young people who need to develop science, technology, engineering, and math skills that will advance space exploration in the future. There was no question—they had to put Mars on the Web.

NASA launched a new website called "Be A Martian" that invites "citizen-scientists" to explore Mars using casual game-like experiences and to assist NASA in classifying the vast number of images in its database. For example, "Mapping Mars" lets citizen-scientists align images from different orbiters, but with the same geo-coordinates, to stitch together a more accurate global map of the planet than computers can achieve alone.

Within two weeks of the site's launch, citizen-scientists had accessed 2.5 million images and were submitting on average 169,000 classifications a day. Be A Martian was a hit.[3]

With such a huge amount of data and a vast number of visitors, how did NASA avoid the dreaded red badge of popularity: "So many people wanted to be Martians that they crashed the site?" Their preventative solution was a very modern one: NASA put the site in the cloud.

The cloud platform handled the large volumes of data as well as spikes in traffic with ease. When the site, which was running on 10 servers, experienced a large spike in visitor traffic right after its launch, site managers made an additional 20 servers available via the cloud—in less than 10 minutes!

---

[3]http://beamartian.jpl.nasa.gov

Cloud Time

Ten minutes in "Traditional IT Time" is akin to "getting it done yesterday"—particularly with a task such as provisioning 20 new servers. You simply cannot fill out a requisition for new hardware, get approval, wait for it to arrive from the vendor, unbox it, plug it in, set it up, make it live, and redistribute your workload in 10 minutes.

But, if you need only 10 minutes to get those servers up and running, what could you do with those weeks in which you no longer need to wait? If you could provision those 20 servers using code instead of people, what else could those people do for your business? If you could rent those servers when you needed their capacity rather than buy and maintain them yourself, what could you do with the money you save?

You could innovate.

CIOs would love nothing more than to flex their innovation muscles and build cutting-edge solutions that do not merely run the business but advance it. If their world could move away from budget constraints and the day-to-day mire of managing existing systems that are sometimes quite old and often complex, CIOs could transform their departments from being the "cost of doing business" to the "engine for growing business." They could be heroes.

Journey to the Cloud

Completing a typical IT task in hours versus weeks or months (and at a lower cost) is one tantalizing promise that has piqued interest in the cloud. In 2010, the Sand Hill Group interviewed 40 cloud leaders and more than 500 IT executives to explore if, when, and how cloud adoption is occurring. They found that 97 percent of respondents had some sort of cloud initiative. Reports from other analysts, such as IDC, have shown that the use of cloud computing is on the rise.

Even so, few are fully convinced. Many of the Sand Hill respondents doubted the ability of cloud providers to offer services that lived up to their marketing claims. Gartner's Hype Cycle from July 2011[4] places cloud computing near the "Peak of Inflated Expectations." How do you separate the truth from the hype? How do you navigate the confusing landscape of cloud providers?

---

[4]Source: Gartner, Hype Cycle for Cloud Computing, 2011, July 2011.

Since migrating some applications can be costly, and since many cloud-based services and tools are in relative infancy, many remain skeptical about the ROI of cloud computing.

Moreover, moving to the cloud does not just affect technology; it affects people. Engineers and operations personnel will need new skills. Development, quality assurance, and release processes will evolve. Some fear for their jobs, while others simply fear any change at all, and their anxieties dwarf any curiosity they might have about the cloud.

We see enterprise CIOs grappling with many of the same questions about how and when to move to the cloud. In this book, we will reassure you that the journey to the cloud need not be decades long, and that adopting cloud services is not an all-or-nothing proposition.

Much of this book is based on Microsoft IT's experience with cloud adoption. We recognize that our enterprise is unique, particularly since we build most of the software we consume. Where we could, we chose to focus on concepts rather than specific technologies. We point out specific technologies, or distinctions among them, when we believe such information is helpful.

No two companies will follow the same process. They will not make the same choices on how to use cloud computing or on which applications to migrate at which point in time. But we can guide you through the learning process, identify areas of exploration, and share details from our own experience. You can start at the beginning of the book, or you can jump in anywhere in the cloud adoption framework we outlined here. You can use this framework as whole, as select parts, or map it to existing enterprise frameworks related to transformation, change management, and systems redesign.

Explore

Cloud computing is a hot topic in the blogosphere, but what exactly is it, and what is its potential? In Chapter 1, "Explore," we decipher enterprise cloud computing and examine its value proposition so you can begin conversations on how your business might take advantage of cloud capabilities.

Envision

So you want to go to the cloud. How do you enlist key stakeholders up to the executive level in the process of identifying where, when, and how cloud technologies might benefit your business? Chapter 2,

"Envision" gives practical advice for developing a business case and building consensus.

Enable

Adopting the cloud will mean changes. How do you get ready? In Chapter 3, "Enable," we explain the pros and cons of various adoption approaches, including which applications you should migrate first, who should do the work, and how you might need to upgrade your organization.

Execute

Delving deeper in Chapter 4, "Execute," we explain how the cloud affects design principles for enterprise architectures, applications, and security. We also examine how development, deployment, and operations activities shift, how to monitor cloud services, and disaster recovery concerns. We close with a discussion of how to measure success and track ROI.

The following diagram, and the drill-down versions at the start of each chapter, is our framework for cloud adoption. They also represent the core concepts covered in this book.

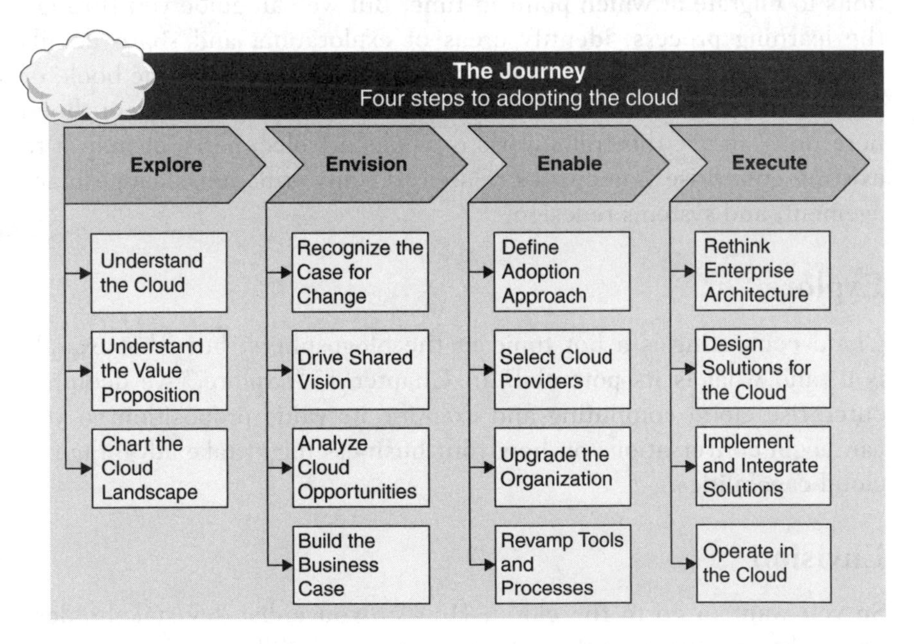

Chapter 1

Explore

Some marketing claims will tout almost anything on the Internet as being "in the cloud." Marketers call services such as web hosting "cloud-based." Others say they are already in the cloud because their internal data center uses virtualization technologies. But for the cloud to live up to its hype, it has to be more than existing technologies (or the Internet itself) rebranded. Like many analysts who are publishing models in an attempt to cut through the noise, we believe there is much more to the cloud.

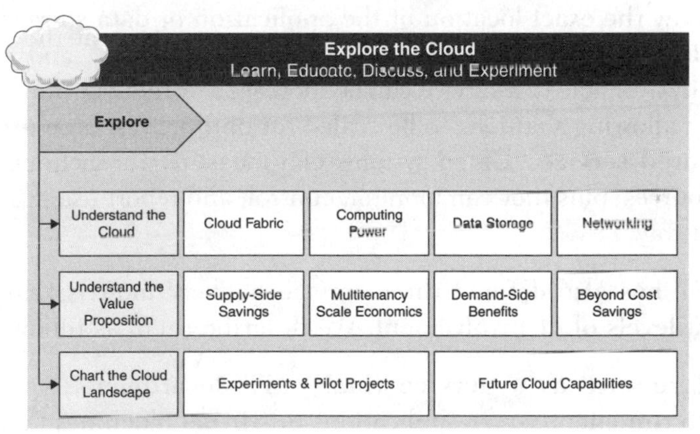

Understand the Cloud

We like the following concise definition put forth by the National Institute of Standards and Technology (NIST):

> *Cloud computing is a model for enabling ubiquitous, convenient, on-demand network access to a shared pool of configurable computing resources (e.g., networks, servers, storage, applications, and services) that can be rapidly provisioned and released with minimal management*

effort or service provider interaction. This cloud model promotes availability and is composed of five essential characteristics, three service models, and four deployment models.[5]

NIST's five essential characteristics of cloud computing provide enough specifics to break the myth that "the Internet equals the cloud." Neither simple web hosting nor virtualized data centers deliver the following comprehensive cloud benefits:

- **On-demand self-service** The service provisions storage and processing power as needed, without human intervention.
- **Broad network access** Mobile phones, laptops, and other devices may access the service using clients such as web browsers or through applications.
- **Resource pooling** Customers share pooled computing resources and data storage ("multitenancy"). Cloud customers may specify where to store data at a macro level (such as geographical region), but they will not know the exact location of the application or data storage.
- **Rapid elasticity** The storage, network bandwidth, and compute capacity available to a service can be increased or reduced almost immediately, allowing solutions to be scaled for optimal resource usage.
- **Measured service** Cloud systems can measure transactions and use of resources, plus they can monitor, control, and report usage in a transparent way.

NIST has also defined three service delivery models that require different levels of IT involvement. We describe them as follows:

- **Infrastructure as a Service (IaaS)** IT departments typically use IaaS to run client/server applications on virtual machines (VMs). The cloud provider manages the network, servers, and storage resources so that IT managers no longer need to buy, track, or decommission hardware. They must still manage operating systems, databases, and applications. Depending on the service provider, they may be able to configure networking components in limited ways. Developers manage configuration remotely via application programming interfaces (APIs) or a web portal, for example, to increase resources to accommodate spikes in demand. Amazon.com's core offering is IaaS. Essentially, it supports virtual machines that customers either develop themselves or select from Amazon's prebuilt library and customize.

[5]Mell, Peter, and Timothy Grance. "The NIST Definition of Cloud Computing (Draft)." http://csrc.nist.gov/publications/drafts/800-145/Draft-SP-800-145_cloud-definition.pdf

- **Platform as a Service (PaaS)** Enterprises use PaaS to develop, deploy, monitor, and maintain applications while the cloud provider manages everything else, including the operating system and middleware. Developers can manage configuration remotely as with IaaS, but they need not build and configure the VM image themselves. Overall, PaaS lowers total cost of ownership (TCO) more than IaaS. Windows Azure is a PaaS offering that introduced scale units known as Web roles and Worker roles, which are abstracted from the underlying VMs. (Windows Azure also includes an offering called VM Role, which, while not branded IaaS, provides some additional flexibility.) Although PaaS generally lacks some flexibility relative to IaaS (for example, unlike Amazon Web Services, Windows is the only option for the operating system layer in Windows Azure), it automates tasks that operational staff must execute manually with IaaS, such as installing operating system patches. In other words, if you select PaaS over IaaS, you trade some control for lower TCO.
- **Software as a Service (SaaS)** SaaS is perhaps the most familiar service delivery model, in which companies subscribe to prepackaged applications that run on a cloud infrastructure and allow access from a variety of devices. Enterprises are rarely responsible for much beyond some configuration and data quality management. Examples include Salesforce.com and Microsoft Office 365.

The following diagram (from "The Economics of the Cloud"[6]) summarizes the three core cloud offerings and who is responsible for management at each layer, relative to traditional IT.

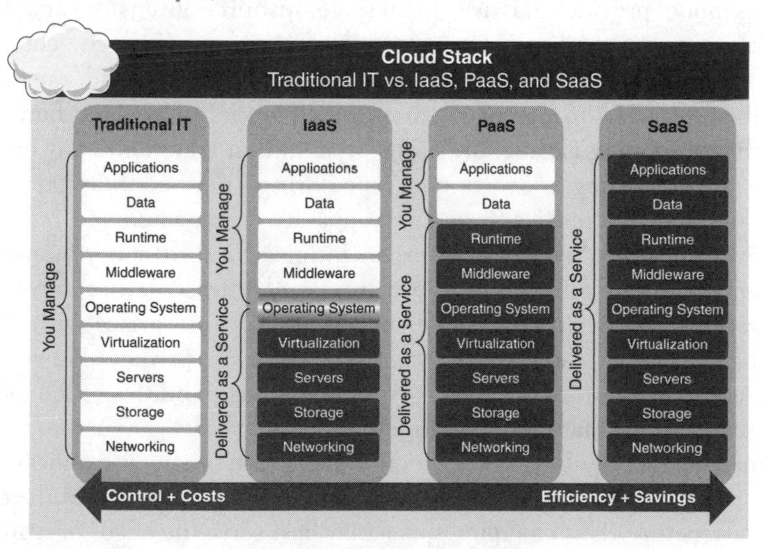

[6]Harms, Rolf, and Michael Yamartino. "The Economics of the Cloud." http://www.microsoft.com/presspass/presskits/cloud/docs/The-Economics-of-the-Cloud.pdf

Chief information officers (CIOs) may also find it worth exploring two emerging categories that complement the NIST definitions:

- **Data as a Service (DaaS)** Through web services and standards such as Open Data Protocol (OData), DaaS provides access to raw data (for example, census statistics) that applications can mine, analyze, visualize, and so forth. The provider manages data quality, while customers have on-demand access at a reasonable cost. Organizations can monetize data by hosting it on cloud platforms such as Windows Azure Marketplace DataMarket.
- **Business Process as a Service (BPaaS)** These offerings represent the next layer of abstraction after SaaS. They provide part or all of a business process, as opposed to a single application, and can even knit together services from multiple vendors. Companies such as ADP, which provides payroll services, have been offering BPaaS for decades. The benefit of the cloud's scale and elasticity makes further growth of BPaaS a development to watch. Furthermore, imagine being able to swap, with relative ease, a vendor delivering part of a business process for another vendor. That is the type of agility BPaaS might provide in the future.

According to NIST, cloud computing environments fall into one of four different models:

- **Public cloud** An organization selling cloud services makes the cloud infrastructure available to a large industry group or the general public. This model provides massive global scale, resource-intensive capabilities such as content delivery networks, and cost savings through economies of scale. Unlike some private clouds, with the public cloud, customers will never need to provision, manage, upgrade, or replace hardware. Although pricing is generally utility-style in that companies pay only for the resources they reserve or consume during a defined time span, some providers also offer fixed-price and capacity arrangements.
- **Private cloud** Whether the organization or a third party manages it on-premises or off-premises, private cloud infrastructure serves one organization. This is the model of choice for enterprises with strong concerns about data security and information privacy. However, it lacks the economies of scale as well as some capabilities (such as geo-replication) of many public clouds.
- **Community cloud** A specific community with common business models, security requirements, or compliance considerations shares the cloud infrastructure. This emerging space may best serve the needs of regulated industries such as financial services and pharmaceutical companies.

- **Hybrid cloud** Two or more clouds (private, community, or public) make up a hybrid cloud infrastructure, but each remains a unique entity linked by technology that enables data and application portability. An example hybrid cloud scenario is cloud bursting for load balancing between clouds.

Moving to the cloud forever changes the IT stack and how it is managed, which means IT itself must adjust. The fundamental shift from a physical world to a logical one, whether for compute or storage workloads, makes the notion of which individual server an application runs on mostly irrelevant. As a result, developers must change the way they architect and write applications. The following diagram illustrates the choices and fundamental characteristics of cloud workloads.

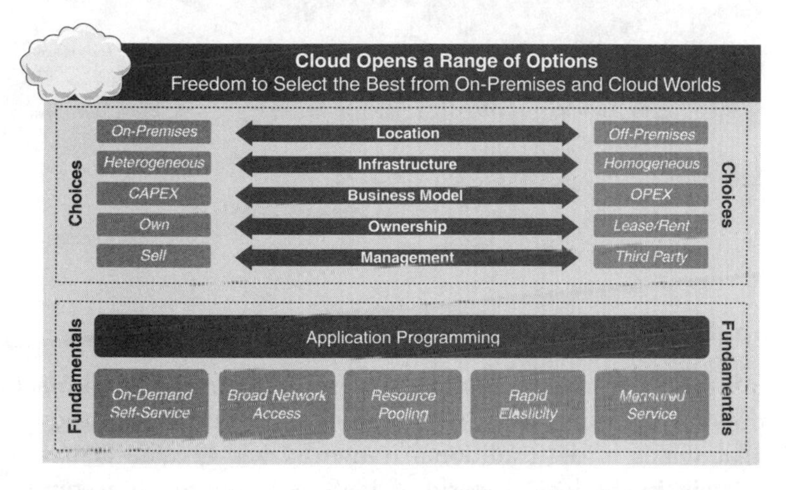

Understanding the building blocks of cloud technologies will give you a better idea of the types of changes your organization may need to make.

Cloud Fabric

The fabric is the software that makes many cloud benefits real, such as scalability and operational savings. A fabric controller serves many of the same functions for a cloud platform that a server administrator does for the traditional enterprise data center: provisioning resources, balancing loads, managing servers, performing operating system updates, and ensuring that environments are available. Capabilities differ from model to model and from one cloud provider to the next. For example, in IaaS the fabric does not automate applying operating system updates. Some of the actions fabric controllers are generally responsible for are outlined in the following illustration:

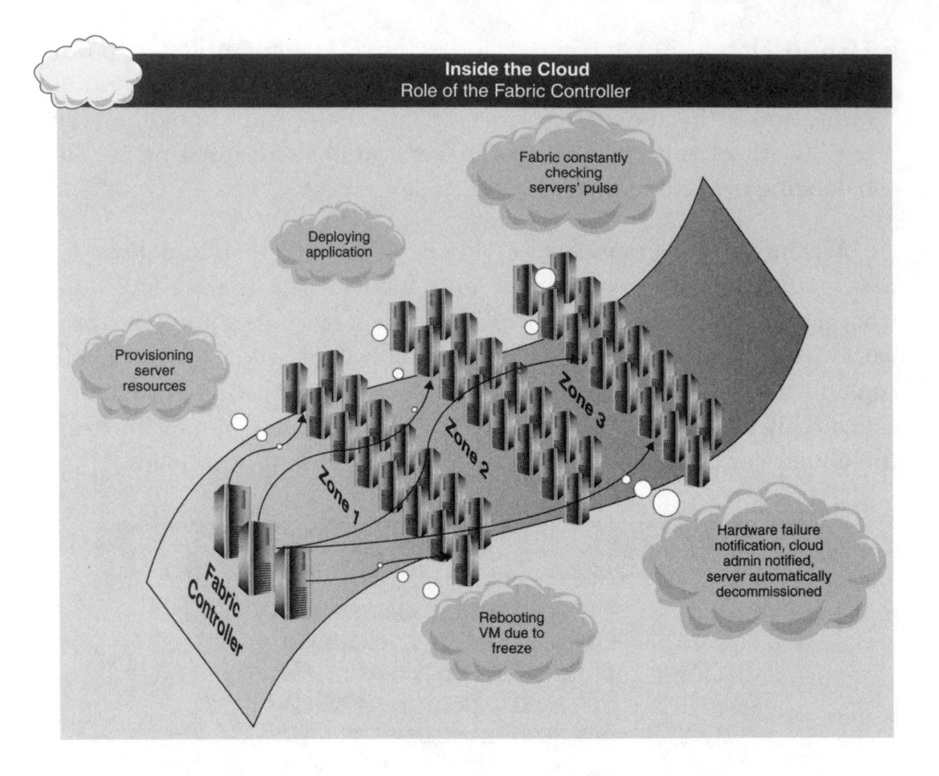

Computing Power

In PaaS and IaaS models, enterprises essentially rent virtual machines that the provider runs on low-cost "commodity" hardware. Although the unit that scales in the traditional nonvirtualized IT data center is the server itself, in the logical world of IaaS, a virtual machine represents a "scale unit." With PaaS, developers "scale out" by spinning up additional instances of an application or one of its components (which are ultimately housed in virtual machines); those instances are the logical scale units. Although developers can "scale up" in the cloud by requesting larger scale units with more processors, memory, and local storage, the real benefit of the cloud is in the ability to "scale out," or add scale units as needed to meet demand.

Data Storage

It is unlikely that the conventional practice of capturing and managing business information in relational databases will go away anytime soon. However, ask yourself whether all of your data truly requires relational capabilities. Moving data to a cloud table service, or even binary large object (BLOB) storage service, may offer significant cost savings, because they are generally less expensive than cloud relational database offerings (which sometimes require paying a premium for SQL technologies). They may also provide performance and scalability benefits. The following summarizes the advantages of each service:

- **Table services** Table services allow data to be stored as individual entities that contain multiple properties (for example, an entity named "Contact" that has "Name" and "Address" as properties). The underlying schema and platform technologies make it possible to store a large amount of data that is still easy to query, even though it cannot be joined across tables as it could be in relational databases. The service can partition data across many servers, enhancing query performance while allowing for an "infinite" data footprint.
- **BLOB storage** Instead of injecting images, videos, or documents into a table, developers can store them as flat files that they can retrieve through web-friendly APIs. Many cloud providers support at least one level of structure, such as grouping BLOBs into a folder. Some, like the Windows Azure BLOB Service, can reduce latency for geographically dispersed users via replication within content delivery networks (CDNs). Use of BLOBs is an important alternative to hosting files directly within a compute scale unit, as all scale units can access BLOBs and persist changes, two operations the virtual machine storage in compute scale units typically do not support.

If your data requires full relational database capabilities, you can use the cloud for SQL services in two ways. The first is to run a SQL database within a virtual machine instance, in which case an enterprise IT manager still manages and maintains the virtual machine, including operating system patches and database software. The second way is to run a cloud-based SQL offering, such as SQL Azure or Amazon Relational Database Service (RDS). Many of the same capabilities available in on-premises versions of databases are present in the cloud, including integration of familiar database management tools. High availability and fault tolerance are typically built into these types of offerings; the cloud provider keeps multiple copies of data on independent servers for redundancy.

Many cloud providers offer additional storage services, such as virtual mounted hard drives for compute instances (which essentially emulate an attached hard drive), to ease the migration path for applications with special storage requirements (for example, if they call file system APIs such as those for NTFS on Windows or EXT3 on Linux). Some cloud storage providers also offer messaging services, such as message queuing, which can behave as short-term storage.

Networking

Cloud providers generally charge for data transfer, which can impact applications that have high bandwidth requirements but minimal compute needs. Providers might not clearly identify the relationship between the number, size, and type of compute scale units and the bandwidth available to each in their pricing model. Because of this, comparing variable costs among cloud providers is challenging, and it is important that you understand how network latency and application "chattiness" could lead to additional costs.

At some point, an enterprise might discover that its network or its Internet connection is causing latency issues, in which case its only option will be to upgrade the connection or hardware (such as web proxy servers). When Microsoft IT took measurements, we also found that software encryption of network traffic can add materially to latency in some cases. This is a consideration when sending corporate traffic over the Internet to a public cloud.

Understand the Value Proposition

You may already be thinking of several ways that cloud computing, with its agility, elasticity, and reduced overhead, could help your enterprise. Let us further explore some of the benefits.

Supply-Side Savings

Electricity has become the largest component of TCO for the enterprise IT infrastructure. In their white paper, "The Economics of the Cloud," Rolf Harms and Michael Yamartino from Microsoft's Corporate Strategy Group explain that large data center operators pay less than a quarter of the national average rate for power because they negotiate bulk purchase agreements and locate facilities where power costs less. Cloud providers also command better pricing for infrastructure components such as hardware and software licenses because they make high-volume purchases.

Even on a small scale, using cloud services saves on labor costs. Thanks to the power of the fabric, one administrator in a cloud data center can manage thousands of servers, while her counterpart in the typical enterprise handles fewer than 200.

Multitenancy Scale Economies

Public clouds take advantage of two cost reduction areas not available to private clouds: demand diversification across industries, and an exponentially larger base of users. According to Harms and Yamartino, public clouds cost 10 times less than private clouds for the same unit of service "due to the combined effect of scale, demand diversification, and multitenancy." Thus, even corporations with a very large base of users and multiple data centers located in different geographical locations could drive down TCO by moving to a public cloud environment.

Public cloud providers amortize the cost of labor and server utilization over a large number of customers. For example, when Harms and Yamartino compared the labor and server utilization costs of Microsoft Office 365 deployed in a private cloud with those of Office 365 deployed in a public cloud, they found that labor costs per customer were far less for the public (shared) offering. Other advantages to using public over private clouds include fewer constraints on scaling (aka "almost infinite" capacity).

Of course, CIOs need to factor in the cost of redesigning existing applications to take full advantage of the cloud (we discuss this in Chapter 2), but a solid analysis will point them in the most cost-effective direction.

Demand-Side Benefits

Because IT must provision hardware in traditional data centers for peak usage scenarios, the majority of available capacity might go unused most of the time. Many companies turn to virtualization as a solution, analyzing demand patterns and adjusting their use of resources. Cloud providers can achieve even lower TCO than most enterprise IT departments, because they can smooth demand variability via multitenancy.

The following table lists the five types of usage variability Harms and Yamartino identify, along with a brief description of how cloud providers are better able to optimize than are IT departments.

Variability Issue	Cloud Optimization
Usage patterns show a certain degree of randomness.	Pooling servers reduces the effects of this variability.
Workplace applications experience predictable peaks based on the time of day.	Global companies can run the same workload on the same servers for multiple time zones. Cloud providers can run different workloads with complementary time-of-day

Variability Issue	Cloud Optimization
	patterns on the same servers, for example, by having consumer and enterprise tenants sharing the same resources.
Industry-specific dynamics drive demand spikes. For example, tax return preparation firms see a spike before major tax deadlines, and e-commerce sites get more traffic before gift-giving holidays.	Most enterprises can increase average utilization from, for example, 5 percent to 40 percent by reassigning idle servers during non-peak periods. Cloud providers can go one step further by diversifying tenants across multiple industries with different peak periods.
Not all business applications use each type of IT resource to the same degree. For example, e-mail applications use data storage heavily, whereas business intelligence modeling needs both data storage and a large amount of compute capacity.	Virtualizing the enterprise data center allows administrators to balance resource usage more easily, but cloud providers have a larger number of possible workload profiles to equalize across available compute, storage, and bandwidth resources.
Buying the right amount of infrastructure to support expected users of an application and predicting growth are two of enterprise IT's classic and perennial challenges.	Data center virtualization helps enterprise administrators diversify workloads on underutilized servers. Cloud services have more users and thus more demand types to spread across available resources.

Beyond Cost Savings

Not only does the cloud lower IT infrastructure and management costs, it provides near-immediate access to high-performance computing that can scale almost instantaneously to the proverbial "nth degree." It makes applications available to employees and customers around the world through many device types, which can be especially transformative in emerging markets, as discussed later in the "Epilogue."

The following table summarizes beneficial changes that come from migrating applications to the cloud.

Change	Effect
Reduced resource needs	Enterprises need fewer resources to perform commodity operational tasks, as cloud providers will manage (and automate) many of them. SaaS requires fewer resources than PaaS, and PaaS requires fewer resources than IaaS.

Change	Effect
Reduced time to market	Provisioning hardware resources takes minutes or hours versus days, weeks, or even months. Because the cloud can scale out almost instantaneously, it is no longer necessary to accumulate and run batch jobs during low peak times; real-time data transfer and workloads processed in parallel versus sequentially will become more commonplace. Developers need not design systems to accommodate technical constraints that are cyclical, such as available server capacity.
Reduced capital expenditures	Cloud computing will shift costs from capital expenditures (CAPEX) to operating expenditures (OPEX) as hardware will be "rented" versus purchased. Predictable cash outflows will replace one-time hits to budgets and corporate balance sheets.
Cost transparency	Traditionally it is difficult to measure the waste associated with a server that is not fully utilized. Usage-based pricing for cloud services makes it easier to track actual IT spend versus projected or estimated spend, even on a per-application basis.
Increased availability	High availability is the default option with many cloud providers, which cloud service level agreements (SLAs) often reflect. The cloud provider can patch host servers (in the case of IaaS or PaaS) or virtual machines hosting a customer's application (in the case of PaaS), and upgrade applications (in the case of SaaS) running in the cloud without customers ever experiencing downtime.
Increased iterative capabilities	Because developers can quickly and easily provision instances, they can favor, without penalty, iterative development, rapid prototyping, earlier user acceptance testing (UAT), and other innovative forms of development over long cycle, waterfall-style methodologies. Of course, the increased agility does not absolve development teams from conducting proper testing and project management; teams should always follow a development methodology. In the cloud, it is easier to employ more rapid development practices.
Increased reach and interconnectivity	The cloud makes it easier to deploy geo-distributed components under a centralized application umbrella with more interconnectivity between platforms, partners, and devices, creating truly global platforms.

Change	Effect
Supercharge other initiatives	The cloud can catalyze simplifying, standardizing, and centralizing an ecosystem, for example, through creating shared services, making it possible to make large-scale changes and not just incremental ones.
Talent recruitment and retention	By shifting focus from infrastructure maintenance to creating business value, IT organizations may be able to attract higher quality talent that is interested in more meaningful and innovative work.
"Unlimited" computing	Although practical constraints such as an enterprise's network bandwidth will still exist, excess capacity should always be available to customers on public clouds, creating the illusion of infinite resources.

Chart the Cloud Landscape

Performing due diligence on all the companies purporting to offer cloud services and consulting might seem daunting; thus, we provide guidance on how to select an appropriate cloud provider in Chapter 3. As you start to experiment with cloud computing, one way to sort out which providers make sense for you is to try out your top candidates. The utility pricing models available through cloud providers make the cost of exploring their offerings relatively small.

Experiments and Pilot Projects

Consider allowing developers to tackle business problems as a way to experiment with using cloud services, as Netflix and Microsoft have successfully done.

Netflix used a boot camp–style approach to move its entire website and other services to the cloud. It isolated software engineers in a space, giving them access to whiteboards, tools, and cloud services, along with the directive to "just get it done." Within two days, the team delivered a working prototype and had already identified tooling issues and bugs to resolve before the new service would be ready for production use.

Microsoft IT created an internal program called the Windows Azure Sandbox to give Microsoft employees and interns a free subscription to Windows Azure and SQL Azure. Developers can use the Sandbox to build proofs-of-concept or prototypes of cloud-based applications.

Ideas they explore in their spare time could potentially lead to the next innovative IT application.

Using the Sandbox to foster collaboration among engineers has resulted in novel solutions to business problems for a relatively small investment of time and dollars. Because developers participating in the Windows Azure Sandbox can solicit near-immediate feedback on proof-of-concept applications and can as quickly release changes, other employees have become more interested in seeing what using cloud technologies can enable. We present a complete case study on the Sandbox in the "Epilogue."

Future Cloud Capabilities

As cloud computing is rapidly evolving, it is important to keep the future in mind as you build your migration plans. Cloud providers will invariably introduce new capabilities that can prompt you to refine your adoption roadmap.

As more enterprises adopt cloud services beyond proof-of-concept or pilot projects, trust in the delivery and deployment models will grow. Cloud standards, including SLAs and compliance with security standards and regulations, will evolve and mature.

Already, cloud providers have automated resource provisioning, scaling, and self-healing. We expect new turnkey solutions, which we refer to as "finished services," for Business Continuity and Disaster Recovery (BCDR) and backup services to emerge. Offerings around caching and identity management will further reduce application development efforts. Providers may also add new levels of support for programming languages, SQL technologies, and operating systems.

Today, many cloud providers do an inadequate job of giving enterprises a holistic view into monitoring and managing resources. Increased use of cloud services will drive the development of better finished services, administrative tooling, and monitoring capabilities. We anticipate that cloud providers will continue to make advances in these arenas and allow operations personnel to define metrics and notifications based on more intelligent definitions of health than "the server is up."

Cloud computing will fundamentally change the approach to workloads. Cloud bursting, the ability to spill over on-premises workloads to cloud environments, will further decouple services from environments. While on-premises and cloud platforms will not have complete feature parity in the near future, portability and integration will become easier, making it possible to "write once" and run on-premises or in the cloud.

We expect the ecosystem of cloud-centric providers, consultants, and systems integrators to develop for a number of years. We will continue to see new SaaS offerings and cloud-based startups. Eventually, a smaller number of providers will end up serving the majority of enterprise customers.

Finally, cloud computing will play an increasing role in green IT initiatives. It makes sense for cloud providers to locate data centers near cheap, renewable sources of power. Even if the cost of energy and raw materials rises, overall energy consumption and costs will decrease as more efficient data centers work at higher utilization rates.

Summary

- According to NIST, the five essential characteristics of cloud computing are on-demand self-service, broad network access, resource pooling, rapid elasticity, and measured service.
- Cloud computing has three service delivery models: Infrastructure as a Service (IaaS), which requires IT to manage operating systems, databases, and applications; Platform as a Service (PaaS), which frees enterprises from managing operating systems and middleware; and Software as a Service (SaaS), which provides prepackaged applications, generally through a subscription.
- Two emerging categories of cloud services are Data as a Service (DaaS), which provides access to raw data; and Business Process as a Service (BPaaS), which provides part or all of a business process, as opposed to a single application, and can even knit together services from multiple vendors.
- Four different models exist for cloud computing environments: private cloud, which serves one organization; community cloud, which serves companies with common requirements; public cloud, which provides massive global scale and cost savings through economies of scale to large industry groups or the general public; and hybrid cloud, which consists of two or more clouds that are linked by technology that enables data and application portability.
- The building blocks of cloud technologies include the cloud fabric, which provisions resources, balances loads, manages servers, and ensures that environments are available; computing power, which consists of virtual machines that can "scale out" to meet demand; data storage, which is available through table services, BLOB storage, and SQL services; and networking.

- The cloud's value proposition includes savings through bulk purchasing agreements for power, hardware, software licenses, multitenancy economies of scale, and higher server utilization; reduced resource needs, time to market, capital expenditures; and increased availability, scalability, and development agility.
- You can try out your top cloud provider candidates, for example, by allowing developers to experiment with proofs-of-concept, to determine which one is right for you.
- It is important that you keep the future in mind as you build your migration plans. Cloud providers will invariably introduce new capabilities that may prompt you to refine your adoption roadmap.

Chapter 2

Envision

Whether your goal for becoming "cloud-powered" is reducing costs or increasing innovation, you will need to create and articulate a clear path from your current state to your future ideal.

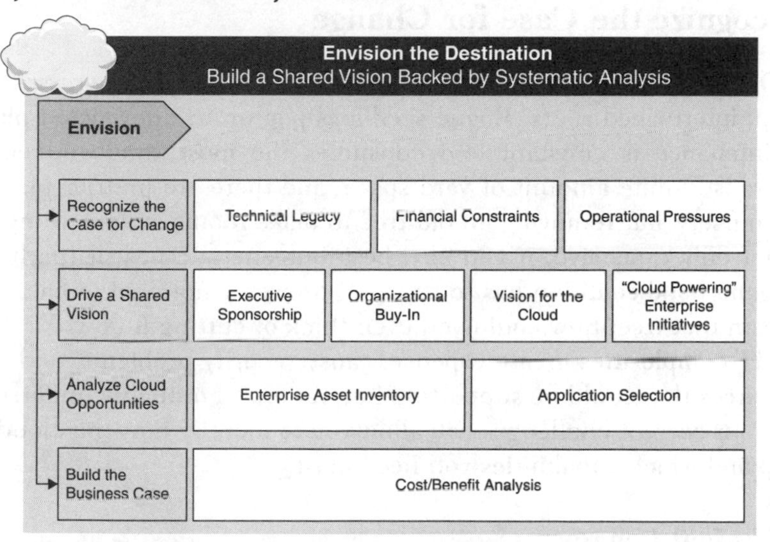

As an executive or professional, you are well aware of the overall health of your company's business and what your leadership believes must happen for it to evolve and grow. What is the mandate for IT?

- *Is real-time data becoming central?* You do not want your supply chain to be caught flat-footed if a celebrity touts your product to the Twitterverse. Real-time data is also essential during crises, such as natural disasters.
- *Has your workforce become more mobile?* If so, your employees need ready access to corporate resources from outside your firewall. You may also need to support a broader array of devices than you have

in the past, particularly as employees request support for consumer devices such as smartphones, tablets, and home computers.
- *Is sustainability a priority?* Green IT is not just about social consciousness; it's about real money. Reducing power consumption to reduce costs or get the most from a limited power supply (as in emerging markets) makes economic sense.
- *Are you moving toward self-service IT?* Software automation is empowering workers to help themselves instead of relying on IT to set up services for them. One example in the area of business intelligence is a self-service portal that allows users to create custom reports directly from a large data store so they will not need a custom IT solution for each query.

Recognize the Case for Change

CIOs are like gardeners. They inherit trees, bushes, and grasses with deep, intertwined roots. Rogue seedlings pop up in unexpected places. Maintenance is constant and consumes the most time and energy. There is a finite amount of yard space, and there are prettier plants at the nursery, but removing an old tree to make room for something new is not only expensive, it can also be a bureaucratic ordeal (perhaps a neighborhood coalition has to approve) or even emotional (a bald eagle lives in that tree; how could you even think of cutting it down?).

IT complexities create expense, cause security problems, and drain resources that could be supporting innovation. Thoroughly understanding your current challenges will allow you to identify how the cloud can help and which capabilities you need most.

Technical Legacy

Every IT department struggles with environments that no one intended to make complex but that simply grew over time into a myriad of platforms, hardware, legacy software, vendors, operational procedures, incompatible architectures, and "spaghetti" ecosystems. Inconsistent configurations at both hardware and software levels proliferate because policies do not exist or compliance is difficult to enforce. What's more, untangling the mess can be difficult because employees who set up systems or wrote the original application code might be long gone.

Older systems tend to be proprietary, with heavy customization. They often manage critical business processes and even more valuable data. Companies get locked in, despite the challenges of maintenance and integration, particularly if deploying an alternative requires significant investments in new hardware, software development, data migration, and training.

Because existing solutions were deployed to solve a problem or address a need, the organization that depends on them does not want to let go lest those problems return or the needs go unmet. It is the proverbial "If it ain't broke, don't fix it" dilemma. Thus, applications live longer than anticipated and are used in ways not originally intended, with more users, functionality, and integrations than originally foreseen.

Financial Constraints

Although examples of IT empowering business growth abound, most CEOs still view it as a cost center or a supplier of services. Thus, they expect year-over-year efficiency increases and cost reductions. Cost pressures constrain system upgrades as well as new development and can create incentives for the risk-averse to pad budgets and timelines, obscuring the true cost of IT.

A culture of cost containment forces IT to plan projects far in advance and prioritize funding requests. Today, most companies, including Microsoft, expense hardware (including servers, storage, and network gear) over some time horizon, such as three years. They may then expense a year's worth of depreciation in a single month. Rather than purchase everything at once, CFOs prefer to spread such IT-related capital expenditures (CAPEX), which are "lumpy" and nonrecurring, across their budget cycle. The result can be projects that are long and drawn-out as purchasing catches up with capacity needs.

Methodical planning can make costs more predictable and controllable, but when a problem or opportunity arises unexpectedly, these controls get in the way.

Operational Pressures

Even sophisticated enterprises can find themselves in constant firefighting mode, unable to get far enough ahead of critical issues to be proactive and directly add business value. Instead, many operational tasks are aimed at simply "keeping the lights on."

Constraints, such as physical limitations on the number of servers IT can maintain in a data center, or slow network links to branch offices, can make even basic operations challenging. The need to respond to externally mandated changes, such as security standards or government financial regulations, adds fuel to the fire.

Organizational inflexibility, including politics, can also squelch proactive efforts. Multiple teams might want to own a new initiative, or competing teams might have trouble collaborating. The personnel or skills necessary to realize a great idea might not exist, and the best talent might not want to be in IT unless they can work on innovative projects.

Drive a Shared Vision

You no doubt have more examples of IT limitations than those described here. Your next step is to map the limitations constraining your organization against the capabilities of the cloud. You might shift only a handful of your portfolio to the cloud, perhaps using Microsoft Dynamics CRM Online to improve customer relationship management and Windows Azure to host a few custom applications, or you might move entire ecosystems to create easier access for strategic business partners as well as employees.

To move forward efficiently, you will need a documented analysis of your application portfolio and a business case for cloud adoption. You will also need to understand the training, resourcing, and organizational transformation that a move to cloud computing will require (covered in Chapter 3).

Executive Sponsorship

As the impact of migrating to the cloud will reverberate across organizational boundaries, buy-in from the leadership team and business units will be essential. Resistance will come from executives who dislike distractions or fear disruption and those who vie for limited resources. If you cannot show them how they will benefit, you may not get far.

When you discuss cloud possibilities with stakeholders from the business units IT supports, consider the following issues:

- **Early adopters** Which stakeholders are most likely to support moving to the cloud, and which are the least likely? Can one or two of them serve as proxies for their broader leadership teams? Could they also offer an application to serve as a concrete example of cloud migration?
- **Funding** From where will funding be obtained for cloud migration? Do you have a direct line to the CFO, or do business units allocate budget to cover IT? Will your leadership support investments necessary across individual applications, such as upgrades to your network infrastructure?

- **Applications** Are stakeholders ready to expand, replace, or retire certain applications? How might the desired changes align with change requests that other business groups might want for similar applications? For example, could you consolidate redundant tools?

While we are aware of the pitfalls of "management by committee," we still recommend convening a group of leaders to oversee your transition to the cloud. Chapter 3 discusses cloud steering committees in depth.

Organizational Buy-In

Even if the cloud's value proposition is evident to many in the business or IT group, selling the change across the organization can take some work. CIOs rallying support for the cloud can face a number of challenges, such as the following:

- **Priorities** Any work performed to ramp up on cloud computing or move applications tends to shift some focus away from adding business functionality or making other IT improvements. Because some may balk at making up-front investments in people and budgets, it is important that you communicate the cloud's long-term benefits, such as lower TCO, increased speed to market, and the ability to free up energy from commodity tasks, and apply it to application innovation.
- **Trust** Stakeholders may question the reliability of cloud technology. They will point out risks, such as degradation of services that are currently working fine, and potential disruption caused by unforeseen migration snafus. They will also be concerned with information security, particularly in public cloud environments. As with any initiative, due diligence and a solid risk mitigation strategy are key to getting stakeholders on board.
- **Dependencies** Stakeholders may have concerns about depending on a third party, particularly with public clouds. They might fear vendor lock-in, since broad cloud standards still do not exist. Some enterprises, such as those in the financial industry, fear they would need to renegotiate contracts if data moves to another environment. Enterprises that must comply with regulations and standards such as Sarbanes-Oxley (SOX) and the Payment Card Industry (PCI) Data Security Standard can find compliance difficult to achieve in current cloud environments.

Getting these concerns into the open is an important exercise. It will guide your analysis and inform your cloud vision.

Vision for the Cloud

A vision document containing an "official cloud policy" will focus your organization, build consensus, and preempt "shadow IT" cloud projects. Developing a cloud vision is, naturally, an iterative process. As you work with stakeholders to identify cloud-worthy projects, be prepared to refine your vision.

Discussions with executive sponsors and business units will determine priorities and timelines. As we explored our cloud options, Microsoft IT interviewed our leadership and business stakeholders to refine our cloud vision. We received these marching orders for our cloud planning:

- *Standardize and be unrelenting.* Too many organizations try to solve the same problems in too many ways. Converge on core platforms, provide a menu of the available capabilities, and mandate their use.
- *Reduce complexity and redundancy.* Do not invent something if you can use processes and systems that are already available. For example, use packaged products wherever possible instead of building custom in-house applications.
- *Fix the "spaghetti."* Determine the best standard architecture for internal systems to ensure stability and performance and reduce redundancy.
- *Improve SLAs.* Achieve higher SLA standards so teams spend less time on troubleshooting and more time on feature releases.
- *Clean up data.* Too many data sources, numerous complicated data feeds, and overly complex tools to channel them make getting to the truth difficult for business owners. Consolidate data and eliminate obsolete data as laws and regulations allow.
- *Do more than just enable technology.* Rather than churning out isolated releases, build a solution portfolio and a roadmap that will have broad business impact.
- *Build on the latest technologies.* Be innovative and progressive. This will also help you develop engineering talent.
- *Fund and prioritize appropriately.* If the IT portfolio does not support the company's strategic priorities, IT should reassess its investments.

"Cloud Powering" Enterprise Initiatives

Every IT department has ongoing initiatives. Rather than viewing cloud adoption as an isolated proposition, you can use the cloud to supercharge or launch other key initiatives.

- **Invest in shared services** The ability to share physical servers is one cloud benefit, but the cloud can do more. Because a cloud scale unit can be more granular than an application (for example, it can be an application component), enterprises can create functional components that can be shared across applications.

  Suppose, for example, that an enterprise has 12 very different applications that all resize high-resolution images at some point. IT could create a single image-resizing component and spin up instances for each application as needed. The component would become part of a library that future applications could use and developers would not have to rewrite.
- **Consolidate global platforms** Some enterprises do not have data centers in certain geographies and do not want to invest in building them. Furthermore, today's definition of a "global platform" is often an application that is hosted in a particular region but accessed by users around the globe. In the cloud, global platforms can become a set of globally hosted, loosely coupled services with a logical architecture, versus a service hosted in a single region but offered broadly. Cloud-based applications can leverage regional data centers and content delivery networks to improve performance.
- **Simplify application portfolios** Migrating an ecosystem to the cloud presents the opportunity to improve it. Enterprises can likely find applications or business processes that they can combine or eliminate altogether during the migration process. They can also reduce complexity, for example, by creating shared services and global platforms or by simply combining a few tools.
- **Improve user experiences** Development teams too often design software applications around technology features rather than the people who use them. People are becoming more reliant on their consumer devices, primarily their mobile phones. They have become accustomed to the ease of use, friendliness, and utility of their consumer applications, and they want the same from IT applications they use to complete work tasks. The cloud's ability to process information on behalf of devices with weaker CPUs (taking advantage of elastic scale), along with the ease of network access available via public clouds, will help IT meet these user expectations.
- **Onboard shadow IT applications** It is not uncommon to discover that shadow applications support important processes in an enterprise. If, in the process of moving these applications to the cloud, IT departments can fold them into the IT portfolio, then support, availability, and services for the applications will improve. Cloud computing's support

for rapid development and utility-style billing can counter fears that cause most shadow projects—those of working with an expensive and bureaucratic enterprise IT group. Coming clean represents a win-win that reduces overall risk.

Analyze Cloud Opportunities

A key aspect of any ambitious business initiative is determining how ready an organization is for change. Can you jump in with both feet and move most applications to the cloud? Or is moving a small portion of the enterprise IT applications your best option? Addressing the following questions is essential to getting cloud-ready.

Business Readiness

- How strong is the relationship between IT and each business it supports? Does your company see, or is it willing to see, IT as a source of competitive advantage?
- Do compliance or contractual issues affect systems?
- Does the business see a potential gain from moving IT to the cloud? Do you have executive sponsorship?
- Do some business priorities need more support? Can the cloud alleviate issues with current systems?

Organizational Readiness

- How up-to-date are the skill sets of your staff? How easy will it be for them to adopt new ways of architecting, writing, and managing applications?
- Do you have good organizational change management processes and tools?
- Will you be able to get the funding and support you need to make necessary organizational changes?

Technical Readiness

- How does your current application architecture compare to the architecture needed to operate in the cloud?
- How many legacy systems, such as mainframe systems, would you need to rebuild?
- Is the current ecosystem adequately supporting business needs and processes? Is IT already due for an upgrade or overhaul?

Enterprise Asset Inventory

An inventory of your enterprise assets should cover the type and age of each application, its architecture, who built it, and who maintains it at what cost. You should note how changes in budget and staffing have affected your ability to maintain and improve these applications.

Be forewarned that good information on your portfolio can be hard to obtain. Even enterprises that keep application information databases can find the information stale, incomplete, or inaccurate. Planning for cloud adoption is a great opportunity to refresh this information and find better ways to track it.

Consider the following questions for a fact-finding survey.

Business Factors

- How critical is this application to the business? How big is the application's user base? Who needs to access it: employees only, or customers and vendors as well?
- How sensitive is the content the application provides or the data it gathers? Would moving it to the cloud raise regulatory or compliance concerns?
- Can the application address future business needs? Are new features planned or requested? Or is the application slated for retirement? If so, when?
- Is the source code available? Do you have access to people who understand it?

Technical Factors: Architecture

- What is the overall architecture of the application? For example, is it a three-tier application? Does it require an installed client, or is it web-based?
- What is the application's platform stack—that is, its operating system and database? Does it use any version-specific capabilities? Is it hosted or dependent on another platform such as Microsoft SharePoint?
- How many integration points does the application have with other systems? How complex are those integrations?

Technical Factors: Data

- What is your best guess on storage needs—that is, application footprint plus data? What kind of non-SQL data (flat file, image, and document) does the application store?

- Can you estimate how many non-SQL storage I/O transactions the application executes per month? For example, how many READ or WRITE transactions occur? (The answer can be important if your cloud provider charges per transaction.)
- What are the historical and projected data growth rates for the application?

Technical Factors: Usage

- Does the application have a predictable usage pattern, or does it have a variable demand profile? Does it experience unpredictable spikes in demand, and, if so, do you know what triggers them? Is usage increasing or decreasing in a measurable way?
- What is your best guess of how much incoming and outgoing bandwidth your application consumes per month to communicate with users and other applications?
- What monitoring needs does the application have? If you have a solution for monitoring existing (on-premises) applications, would it work for cloud-based deployments?

As you review survey results, identify opportunities to simplify applications or to consolidate functionality into shared services as you move to the cloud.

From our survey of application owners, Microsoft IT identified a large number of potential candidates for migration to Windows Azure. Approximately half the applications that respondents maintained were fully web-based, interacted with two or fewer other applications, and had periodic spikes in demand. In addition, most applications (particularly less critical ones) used less than 40GB of SQL Server storage.

Application Selection Process

The following flowchart illustrates the high-level process Microsoft IT used to evaluate which applications to move to the cloud and in what order. We disqualified some applications at the outset, such as those that we planned to retire in the near future or that could not easily meet regulatory requirements in the near term if deployed in the cloud. We then identified applications that were viable candidates, for example, because their demand patterns maximized cloud benefits. Finally, we put them in priority order.

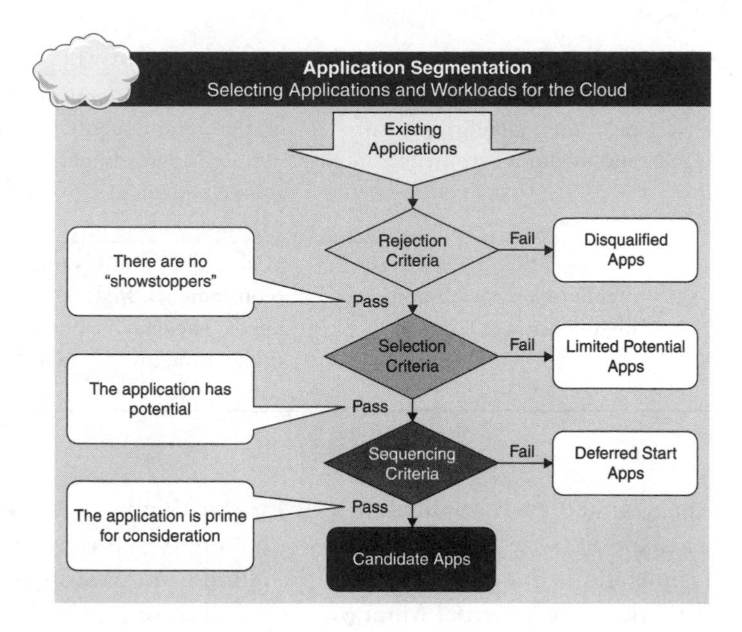

Categorization

Some types of applications are better suited to the cloud at its current level of maturity. When Microsoft IT categorized our applications, we weighed risk and sensitivity, measuring how critical the application was to running our business, its level of regulatory exposure, and the sensitivity of information it collects and stores.

On the technical side, we rated the complexity of the solution design, its monitoring needs and database size, and whether we had access to the source code. Based on our survey, we created three application segments: Basic, Intermediate, and Advanced. Keep in mind that "low," "medium," and "high" as used in the following table are relative terms. Microsoft's definition of "low" will be different from that of a financial or pharmaceutical company. You will need to define your own scale customized for your environment.

We "prequalified" applications in the Microsoft IT portfolio by ranking them according to the application segmentation criteria shown in the following table:

Category	Business Criteria	Technical Criteria
Basic	Not mission-critical, with limited regulatory exposure and low-sensitivity content	Low cross-premises integration requirements, low monitoring needs, accessible source code, and < 10GB database storage

Category	Business Criteria	Technical Criteria
Intermediate	Not mission-critical, with medium regulatory exposure and medium-sensitivity content	Medium cross-premises integration requirements, medium monitoring needs, accessible source code, and < 50GB database storage
Advanced	Mission critical, with high regulatory exposure and high-sensitivity content	High cross-premises integration requirements, high monitoring needs, packaged application integration, and > 50GB database storage

We then ranked each application's fit for the Windows Azure platform on a scale of 1 to 5. Based on the preliminary score, we recommended applications that could move to the cloud using Windows Azure Web and Worker roles, Virtual Machine (VM) roles, or a hybrid model, which would leave some components on-premises.

We recommend a "cloud first" policy for all new applications that can be hosted in the cloud. At the very least, they should be designed for easy migration. Although the percentage of new enterprise applications is generally in the single to low double-digits relative to an existing application portfolio, the ROI case for building them in the cloud, once any constraints get addressed (such as security or regulatory concerns and operational readiness), is often a slam-dunk.

Demand Patterns

Determining which applications are the best fit for the cloud requires analyzing user demand and usage patterns, as well as workload characteristics. Applications with the usage patterns described in the next few pages will benefit more from cloud capabilities and will frequently achieve larger cost savings than applications with relatively flat usage patterns.

Predictable Bursting Applications that manage budget or sales operations need considerably more resources at the end of each quarter or fiscal year than they do the rest of the year. Instead of provisioning, reserving, and continually paying for excess capacity to accommodate the peak load scenario, IT can use cloud computing to scale out during peak loads and scale down when fewer resources are necessary. This way, enterprises pay only for what they use, and this can result in considerable savings.

Other examples of seasonal fluctuations that affect application loads include limited-time marketing campaigns such as specials on pizza ordered online during Super Bowl Sunday, last-minute filing of tax returns close to the government deadline, or holiday periods when gift purchases soar. Numerous Microsoft IT applications fit this category, particularly those supporting the release of new products. Core services, such as e-mail and collaboration, often fit this category and are good Software as a Service (SaaS) candidates due to their commodity nature. A predictable bursting pattern is illustrated as follows:

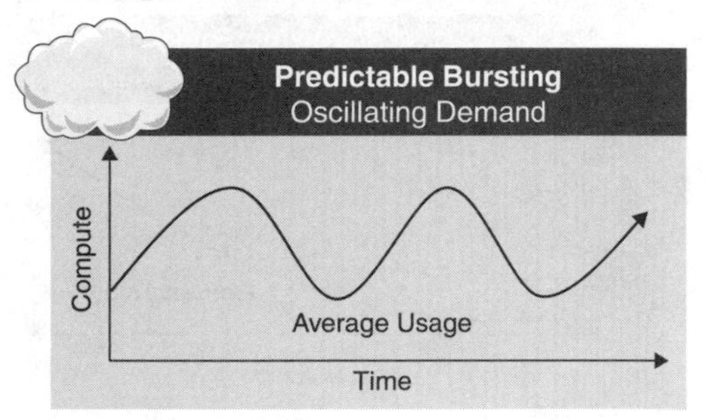

Unpredictable Bursting The cloud's agility enables quick scaling for unpredictable demand scenarios. Word of "something cool" spreads like wildfire over the Internet, sometimes leaving IT departments unprepared. (For example, when the Centers for Disease Control (CDC) published a page on how to survive a Zombie Apocalypse,[7] it received so many hits that the servers crashed.)

Other examples of unpredictable demand include crisis management, such as when people use social networking to find friends and loved ones after a natural disaster; more shoppers responding to an advertised deal about a hot new product; or when IT launches a new tool not knowing what user demand to expect. An unpredictable bursting pattern is illustrated as follows:

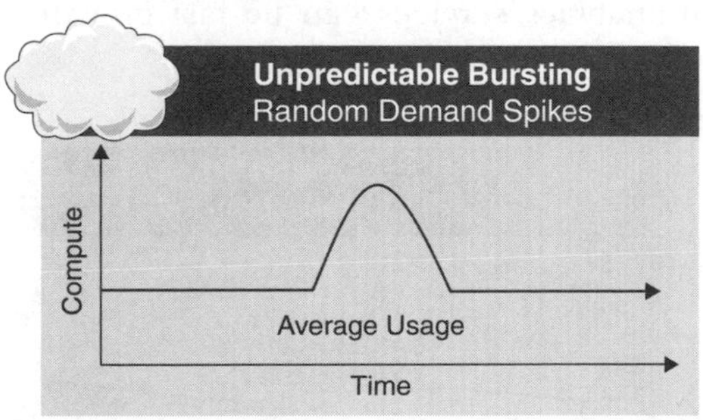

[7]Khan, Ali S. "Preparedness 101: Zombie Apocalypse." CDC. http://emergency.cdc.gov/socialmedia/zombies_blog.asp

Growing Fast The lead time required for expanding data centers to accommodate usage growth constrains enterprises. Cloud computing mitigates this issue, as scaling out takes mere minutes or hours. The scenarios for fast growth can be similar to those of unpredictable bursting. Rather than peak, however, loads continue to grow. Social networking sites that quickly find an enthusiastic audience and gain popularity through viral adoption are good examples of fast growth services. A growing fast pattern is illustrated as follows:

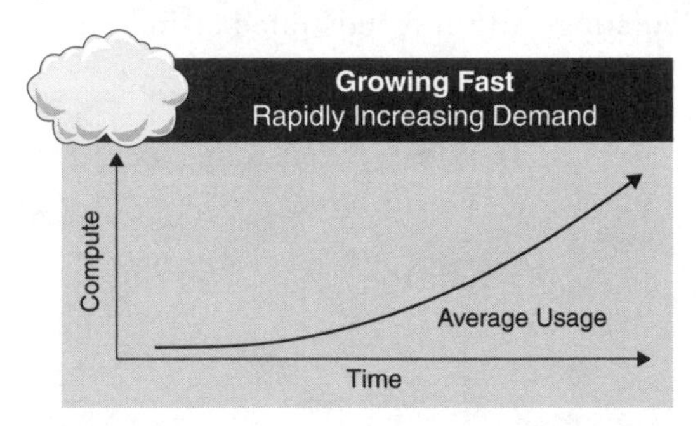

On and Off Instead of paying for and maintaining an infrastructure year-round, using the cloud, enterprises can suspend services when applications are out of cycle or scale them down to a minimal footprint. Applications in this category can scale out once, twice, or a few times a month—for example, for those managing end-of-week timesheets or payroll processing. Some applications may be used heavily only once or twice a year, such as those for employee performance evaluations or benefits enrollment. Still others, such as event registration sites, may be used on an irregular basis. Analytics applications that analyze large data sets may fit this category, although these applications often fit more than one category (that is, financial-related or sales-related analytics applications may have cyclical patterns related to quarter or year's end; newly launched analytics services can be fast growth). An on and off pattern is illustrated as follows:

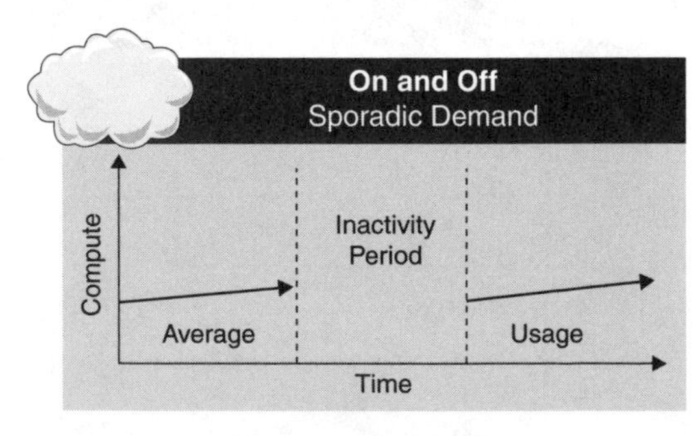

Additional Scenarios Several additional application scenarios are worth considering as cloud adoption candidates. They have usage and demand patterns that are suitable for the cloud.

- **Overflow** Enterprises might want to keep an application on-premises but could benefit from allowing excess demand to spill over to a cloud instance. This is called "cloud bursting." Applications that periodically engage in compute-intensive activities, such as financial analysis or research modeling, may fit this category.
- **Archiving** Enterprises can use the cloud to store and retrieve archived data for on-premises applications. Using the cloud will yield benefits, such as minimizing infrastructure-related efforts around creating and managing archive environments, whether the data is accessed frequently or infrequently. Of course, archiving data can also improve performance in some applications.
- **Storage** Exceptionally large data storage scenarios, such as data warehousing, can take advantage of the cloud's scalability and inherent redundancy whether the data is relational, nonrelational, or consists of flat files.
- **Partnerships** The cloud can benefit partner and joint-venture scenarios by serving as a central point of systems integration for both parties. Demand can be unpredictable in partnership scenarios, and a public cloud can be a ready-to-use platform for hosting applications that all partners access.
- **Industry-specific** The notion of a community cloud specializing in applications for a particular industry could become more commonplace. Such offerings could cater to industry-specific needs, such as compliance with financial or pharmaceutical regulations, while taking into account cyclical demand patterns.
- **Failover** The cloud can provide backup and redundancy for on-premises applications. Kelley Blue Book, for example, uses Windows Azure as a "backup site" for its on-premises kbb.com. If its main site ever goes down, the application directs user requests to the Windows Azure instance.[8]

Build the Business Case

Once you have an idea of which applications you can migrate to which type of cloud environment (public, private, or hybrid), you should be able to start building a business case for cloud migration: how much it

[8] "Microsoft Case Study: Kelley Blue Book." http://www.microsoft.com/casestudies/Case_Study_Detail.aspx?casestudyid=4000005874

will cost, how long it will take, what resources it will require, and how you will measure ROI.

Cost/Benefit Analysis

You will need to start with a baseline of your current hardware, development, operations, and support expenses for the applications you consider good cloud candidates. The financial projection for the cost of moving those applications to the cloud should not only quantify investment costs, but it should quantify potential cost reductions, cost avoidance, and revenue impact.

- **Application development and maintenance** Development and test productivity increase with on-demand environments. There is less need to configure environments and less chance of variability among them.
- **Support labor** IT is no longer responsible for infrastructure operations such as server deployment and configuration, software patching and upgrades (with PaaS and SaaS), and many forms of incident management when servers and storage move to the cloud.
- **Hardware and hosting** Server and storage utilization is higher in the cloud than on-premises. Multitenancy with other customers, if an acceptable option, creates economies of scale that can lower costs even further. There is also less need to plan for scalability from a hardware perspective.

Consider the following points when communicating the cost savings of your cloud strategy:

- Demonstrate that the cloud can save your enterprise money long-term, even when accounting for upfront migration costs.
- Explain that CAPEX becomes OPEX, smoothing out IT spending over time. Discuss and align with your CFO or finance counterparts about the implications of the change from a predetermined budget to a pay-as-you-go model.
- Determine whether a public cloud strategy is a viable alternative to a private cloud to achieve better savings.
- Advocate consolidation and simplification of existing solutions so that IT can focus on innovation.

The following diagram illustrates how Microsoft IT determined it could benefit from savings that the cloud offers. “Addressable spend” refers to that portion of the IT budget that moving to the cloud can impact. (It will have little to no effect on some cost areas, such as desktop procurement.)

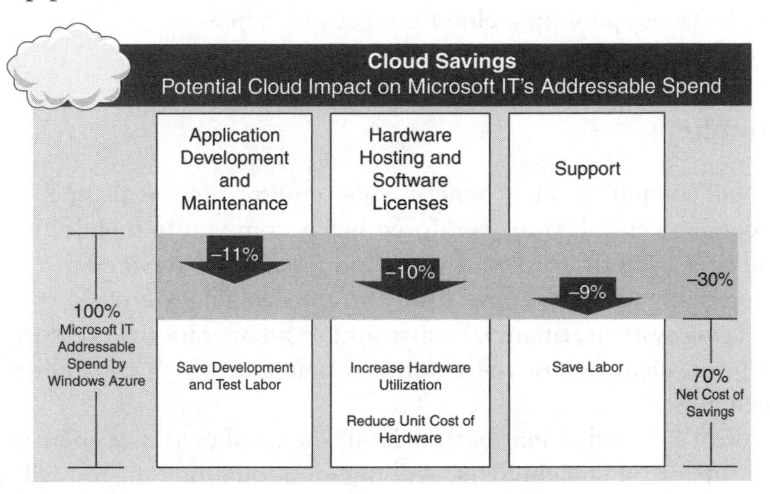

The more applications an enterprise develops in the cloud, the greater the overall benefits and savings, as shown in the following table:

	Addressable Spend	Impact
Development	Cost of developing and maintaining applications	Increased developer productivity; faster, more responsive app development
Integration	Cost of multiple integration technologies, legacy architectures, sustainability	Integration easier over time through scalability and standardization
Security	Cost of maintaining enterprise security	Security concerns heightened initially, but costs now partly borne by cloud provider
Hardware	Cost of procuring hardware for new applications or upgrades for existing hardware	Reduces need to procure incremental hardware
Software Licenses	Ongoing cost of software licenses	Reduces number of software licenses required; often built into cloud pricing
Operations	Cost of running data centers, including utilities and personnel	Reduces need to operate data centers
Support	Cost of end user and application support	Standardization of environments and reduced operations responsibility lowers occurrence of issues and therefore costs

In addition to cost-benefit analysis, proofs-of-concept and pilots can increase stakeholder trust and counterbalance unwarranted skepticism. We will discuss piloting a cloud project in Chapter 3.

Summary

- Cloud computing may benefit your enterprise if real-time data is becoming central, your workforce has become more mobile, sustainability is a priority, or you are moving toward self-service IT.
- Thoroughly understanding your current challenges around complexity, aging systems, financial constraints, and operational pressures will help you identify how the cloud can help and which capabilities you need most.
- To drive a shared vision for the cloud, you need executive sponsorship, the support of stakeholders, and organizational buy-in. You will need to address issues around available funding, investment priorities, and cloud computing risks.
- You can use the cloud to supercharge existing IT initiatives by investing in shared services, consolidating global platforms, simplifying application portfolios, improving user experiences, and on-boarding shadow IT.
- Take an inventory of your enterprise applications to understand their business impact, architecture, data properties, and usage patterns.
- You will need to determine which of your applications are suitable for the cloud (by analyzing demand patterns, for example) and then prioritize the applications according to business and technical criteria.
- Your business case should quantify investments, cost reductions, and revenue impacts in the areas of application development, labor, hardware, and bandwidth.

Chapter 3

Enable

By now you have identified ways your enterprise could benefit from using cloud services. The next step is to decide how to move forward.

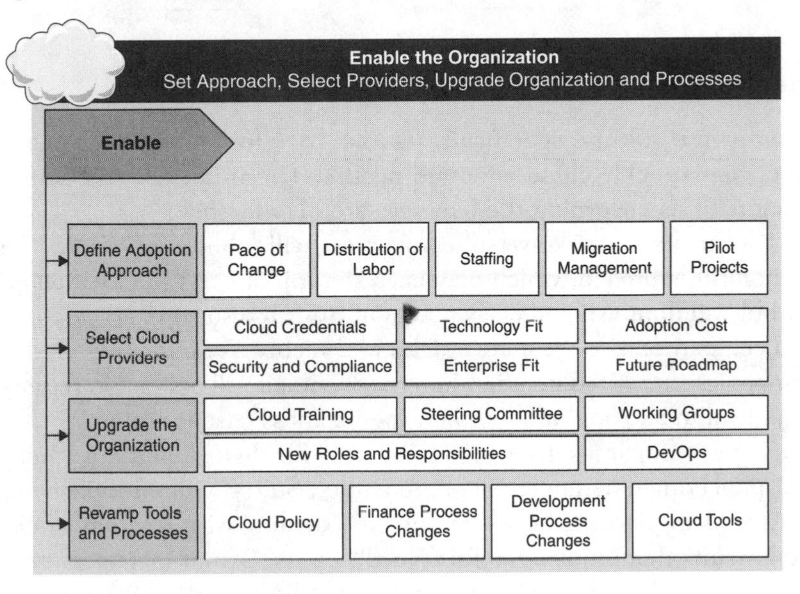

Define Adoption Approach

To move forward effectively, your organization will need a defined approach to cloud migration that clarifies who will make key decisions, how aggressive your migration timeline is, how your timeline will affect staffing, and whether the leadership will enact tight controls or support experimentation at the grassroots level. Depending on the size and complexity of your organization and the business pressures your enterprise is facing, you may choose a more conservative, or gradual, adoption approach; a balanced approach; or an aggressive approach. The implementation characteristics related to these approaches, which are also discussed further in this section, are summarized in the following illustration:

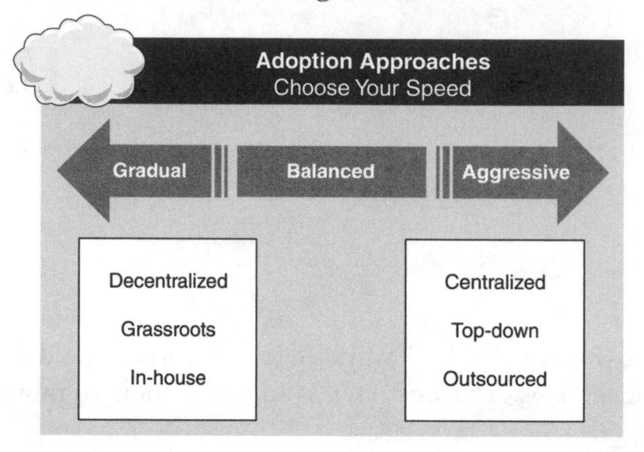

Pace of Change

A company's culture, specifically its tolerance for change, will naturally affect how quickly cloud adoption occurs. The number and complexity of regulations governing the business are also factors.

Executives at risk-averse companies will choose a slower, more methodical approach, which may keep the initial costs of cloud adoption low but will diminish and delay potential ROI. It also leaves the door open for a competitor to move more quickly and secure a competitive advantage. Companies interested in a first-mover advantage will act fast in rethinking IT and will make bold moves when the business case is strong.

Some companies have good reasons for being cautious. Imagine a hospital conglomerate based in the United States with multiple complex IT systems in place. Its legal team is busy dealing with a variety of claims and lawsuits that require careful recordkeeping. Senior management worries about making a significant change to the way the hospital collects and stores patient information. They are concerned about how relying on cloud providers will affect regulatory compliance and accreditation.

A financial consulting firm may fall on the other end of the spectrum. Say the firm manages funds for corporate and individual investors. Customer demand for access to account information through a variety of devices is growing, but the firm's applications were developed in silos and customers complain about slow performance and missing features. The executive team is concerned they will lose accounts to competitors if they cannot meet customer expectations—and quickly. An aggressive approach makes sense for this firm, even though it must address regulatory and privacy concerns when making any changes.

In reality, the picture is rarely as clear as it is for these two fictitious companies. CIOs will find the business cases different for different portions of their application portfolio. Using your segmented application inventory and business case as a guide, determine which applications could be moved to the cloud quickly. Include these applications as part of a multi-wave plan as shown in the following illustration:

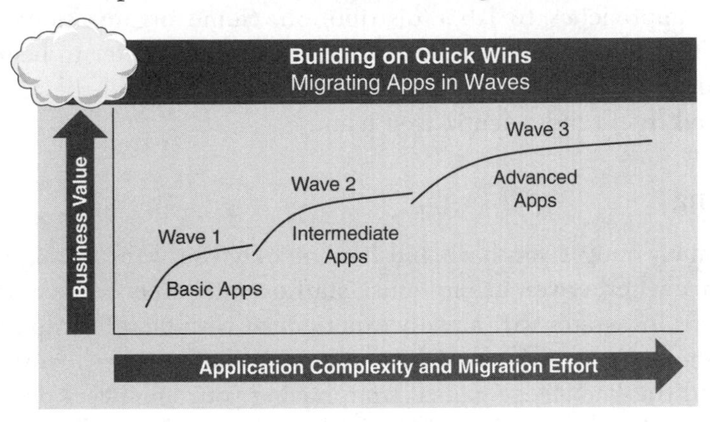

Quick wins are critical for building momentum inside your organization and calming naysayers. Determine whether more complex applications can be refactored. Find out if it is possible to build shared services to replace on-premises applications after existing contracts or licenses expire. Finally, consider whether it is feasible to implement a "build all new applications using cloud services" policy.

Distribution of Labor

The work of migrating applications to cloud services can follow the established distribution of labor in your company. However, it might be easier to adopt cloud services by stepping outside the norm.

In decentralized organizations, multiple teams are involved in planning, delivering, and operating services, and teams working directly with affected business units make decisions. Although distributed teams may have better business knowledge of applications, the decentralized model might not be as efficient for mass migrations or consolidating services.

In a centralized model, a dedicated team manages the full IT lifecycle, in this case, for cloud computing. All business units share their requirements with this team. Decision-making, funding, and resourcing are all centralized. In this model, the centralized team may lack application-specific knowledge, but it works well when mass-migrating simple applications, as repeatable processes and reusable tools can maximize efficiency. Identification of reusable application components and automation of administration tasks are natural outcomes of a centralized "migration factory" approach.

While the up-front investment may be greater, the centralized model improves payback with better application selection and more consistent implementation. Another option is to combine centralized and decentralized approaches to labor distribution. Some organizations find it difficult to start out with a centralized team. They prefer to begin with small distributed teams, achieve initial success to build their business case, and then fund a centralized team.

Staffing

How much budget you have and how quickly you want to migrate will influence whether you use in-house staff or outsource to consultants or a systems integrator (SI) already experienced with cloud computing.

In-house resources need less ramp-up time on the business context, and the knowledge gained from having your engineers design and implement for the cloud stays inside the company. You will also be able to manage the development of standards and patterns more directly. On the other hand, internal teams must balance cloud migrations against their other work and may need training in cloud computing.

Hiring consultants who already have cloud computing skills can jumpstart your migration, giving your IT teams more time to build their cloud competencies. IT and business unit employees with deep domain knowledge can learn cloud practices as they work with vendors to develop scenarios and test proofs-of-concept, ensuring that the results meet the needs of the enterprise.

As with distribution of labor, consider a combined approach. You might want to seed a small team to start experimenting with the cloud and augment them with vendor resources. Your current vendors already know something about your business and may have teams of cloud experts who can ramp up quickly because of your preexisting relationship. The right mix of in-house and vendor resources for your business depends heavily on existing expertise and the current balance of in-house versus outsourced applications.

Migration Management

A top-down approach allows senior managers to steer the migration approach and promotes consistency in tools, processes, and application architecture. It also helps ensure that intersecting groups, such as engineering and operations, stay aligned and makes course corrections easier. The danger is bureaucracy. Senior management has to approve the business case for moving a segment of applications, changes to policies and procedures, and recommended cloud providers. Office politics can interfere as managers weigh cloud adoption against other business initiatives that compete for funding and resources.

Bottom-up tactics can build grassroots enthusiasm for cloud computing at a relatively low cost. For example, it costs Microsoft IT only a few dollars per month for a developer to participate in the Windows Azure Sandbox. Inadvertent consequences can arise with a bottom-up approach, however, such as competing solutions to the same problem, lack of standardized architectures or coding practices, or proliferation of shadow IT projects. If no senior managers pick up the cloud computing flag, cloud engineering may not progress beyond a mere extracurricular activity.

Based on Microsoft IT's experience, we think that enterprises serious about their cloud journey can make strong progress by establishing top-down control while allowing for bottom-up experimentation that can generate valuable learning, best practices, and innovative projects.

The case for top-down governance is made even stronger considering that cloud computing is rapidly evolving. There are numerous vendors and platforms with varying capabilities and a lack of standardization across the industry. The scenario most CIOs want to avoid is one that many have already experienced: fragmented tools, processes, and platforms that add both cost and operational complexity. Strong top-down governance will help.

Pilot Projects

Fast or slow, centralized or decentralized, in-house or outsourced, managed top-down or encouraged from the bottom up, the best way to learn what will work in your enterprise is to do pilots. Pilot migrations can help fill technical knowledge gaps, test whether expected benefits can be realized, and provide cost-savings data. You can start small with one or two noncritical applications that have a modest level of demand, as well as one application that is large and complex.

Early in our evaluation process, Microsoft IT identified our internal charitable Giving Campaign Auction Tool,[9] shown in the following illustration, as a good pilot.

[9]"Microsoft IT Moves Auction Tool to the Cloud, Makes It Easier for Employees to Donate." Microsoft Case Studies. http://www.microsoft.com/casestudies/Case_Study_Detail.aspx?CaseStudyID=4000005933

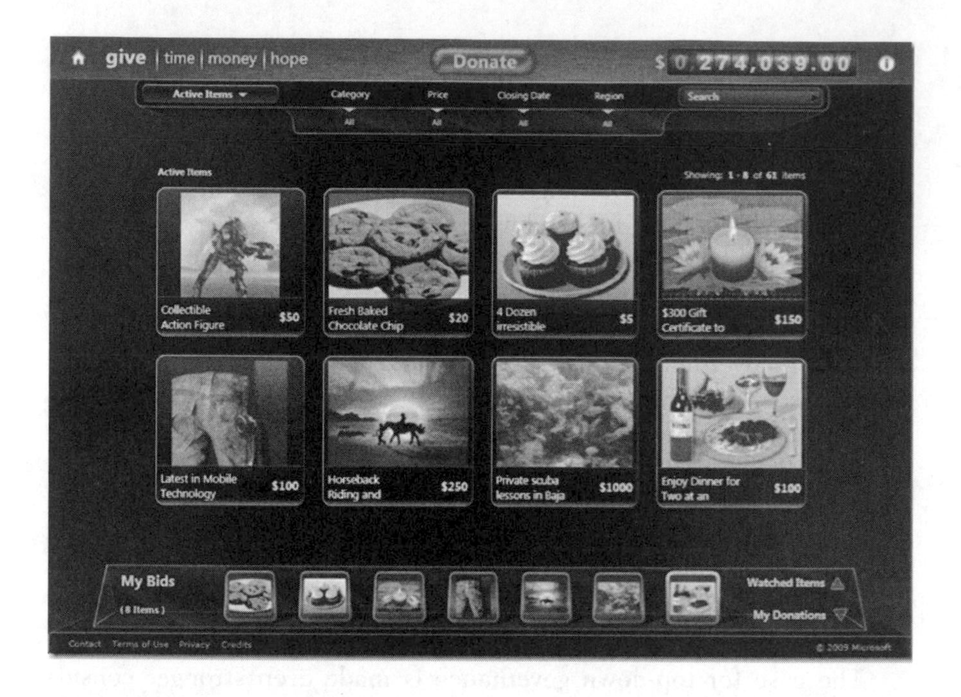

Microsoft runs its employee giving campaign every October. In addition to making cash donations, employees donate goods and services for an online auction. For years, the servers that hosted this site were underutilized except during October, when utilization reached its peak. The auction tool's usage profile is, therefore, a combination of "on-off" and "predictable bursting" patterns well suited for the cloud.

Moving the auction tool to Windows Azure resulted in a new fundraising record, not just because its migration to the cloud created buzz, but because additional capacity was always available to meet user demand. Bidders experienced no performance slowdown as the number of scale units increased sixfold during the final bidding frenzy. The tool took less than two weeks to migrate from on-premises to Windows Azure. Successes like this one have helped Microsoft IT build momentum to move forward with redesigning higher demand applications, some with far more complex feature sets.

Assuming proper funding, we predict most enterprises can move their first few applications to cloud services in a matter of months. The results from these early experiences will provide important insight that can help refine your company's migration strategy, for example, helping you adjust the pace. They can also increase your organization's interest and excitement about using cloud services.

Select Cloud Providers

Before you select providers, you need to determine what mix of Software as a Service (SaaS), Platform as a Service (PaaS), and Infrastructure as a Service (IaaS) is appropriate for your portfolio.

Companies can take advantage of SaaS right away for widely used, commoditized services such as e-mail and productivity applications. IaaS can produce quick savings without costly re-architecting for applications that require older operating systems or components. It is also a good fit for applications dependent on software that takes a long time to install or cannot be installed via a script. (With IaaS you can preinstall these components on the base image, which might not be possible with PaaS.) Moving such applications to PaaS would involve the higher up-front cost of refactoring them to function fully in the cloud, but redesigning and/or modernizing applications for PaaS can also provide long-term savings from more efficient operations and reduced maintenance.

The process of choosing a cloud provider is not much different from the process of selecting any vendor. The services the provider offers, how long it has been in business, the maturity of its business processes, the thoroughness of contracts and SLAs, and how clearly and completely its representatives answer your questions all matter when selecting cloud companies. Several types of cloud providers and offerings are shown in the following illustration:

Cloud Provider Landscape
Categories of Cloud Companies

Company Type	Offerings	Examples
Cloud Technology Provider	Creates cloud technology, including cloud software stacks. In many cases, these firms are also cloud service providers.	Microsoft, Amazon, Google, Salesforce, VMware
Cloud Service Provider	Provides cloud products, hosts cloud services, or both; may or may not build all the underlying technology themselves.	Fujitsu, Dell, HP, Rackspace
Cloud Independent Software Vendor (ISV)	Offers value-add services for clouds, including managing or monitoring. Could also include building value-add services or applications on top of clouds.	RightScale, CiRBA, enStratus, ScaleXtreme, Canonical
Cloud Systems Integrator (SI)	Assists companies in implementing applications on clouds.	Accenture, Infosys, TCS, Wipro

Enterprises might opt for multiple cloud providers or platforms within or across the SaaS, PaaS, and IaaS categories. Although most providers adhere to some level of web standards, there are currently no clearly defined industry protocol standards for cloud services. For the foreseeable future, it is important that you understand the integration story of cloud providers and what aspects of their platform are proprietary. Programming APIs for languages available on-premises today generally carry over between providers, but be aware of possible API-level exceptions. However, the APIs used to access cloud-specific services from the Web, such as for scaling or storage, are generally inconsistent among providers.

Cloud Credentials

Odds are, you can easily rule out some "cloud" providers just from their marketing materials. Look for the following:

- Do they offer usage-based pricing models? If they offer only fixed pricing arrangements, they might be "cloud-washing"—that is, rebranding traditional web applications without offering true cloud functionality, such as on-demand scaling, resource pooling, rapid elasticity, and metering.
- How often do they perform service updates? If their changes to improve features or tighten security happen only once or twice a year, the firm is likely still using traditional software development methods—a sign it is not yet a true cloud provider.
- Do they offer resource pooling across tenants? If they deploy one cloud instance per customer, they are not offering true shared public SaaS or PaaS.
- Can customers add or remove compute capacity or storage on-demand? True cloud providers offer both capabilities as well as tools that support self-service provisioning.
- Do they provide usage data? Not having the ability to track usage data in a utility pricing context exhibits a lack of "cloud thinking" and makes it difficult for customers to optimize operations.

Technology Fit

Once you have identified a true cloud provider, you will want to look more closely at their supported technologies, including which tools they provide to support application migration, monitoring, and manageability.

Unless they support the underlying operating system stacks (such as Windows or Linux) and technologies you need to transition without doing major rewrites, you should consider the provider only if you already expect to redesign your applications or expect long-term benefit for doing so.

If the provider uses mostly proprietary technology (for example, the way Salesforce's Force.com uses their Apex programming language), you then need to evaluate whether the features address enough of your company's business needs to risk vendor lock-in.

If the provider's cloud is built on preexisting technology (as with Microsoft and Amazon) and integrates with many existing tools, the learning curve for developers and operations personnel will be less steep thanks to familiar toolsets and software development kits (SDKs).

Adoption Cost

Pricing models for cloud computing continue to evolve, and it can be a challenge to make an "apples-to-apples" cost comparison. Consider the following:

- What does the provider charge for compute, storage, and bandwidth usage?
- Does the provider charge for customer support? Can you easily add or remove levels of support?
- Are there costs involved with setting up and maintaining user accounts for a SaaS offering?
- Do PaaS and IaaS providers offer training or consulting to help you get started? Can you access SDKs, developer tools, and other helpful technical documentation for free?

You will also need to consider costs that may arise independent of the provider you select, such as general network and network edge service upgrades, new tools or processes, or consultants.

Security and Compliance

Moving services to a public cloud means potentially increasing your business's exposure to malicious attacks. It is important to determine how well a cloud provider handles both technical and legal issues, and how your enterprise will be affected should problems arise. Our advice when selecting a cloud provider is this: Know what you contracted for and what you are getting into and consider the following:

- What physical controls does the provider have in place to protect their data centers? Do they conduct background checks on their employees?
- Which tools do they use to detect intrusion? Do they offer anti-malware or antivirus services?

- Do they offer access to detailed administrative logs or other data needed to establish audit trails for compliance purposes?
- Does their data center and service have any of the following certifications: ISO/IEC 27001, SOX, HIPAA, or PCI/DSS? Have they attained auditor statements, such as SAS 70 Types I and II?
- Do their cloud services support native encryption of data at rest and data in motion?
- Is it possible to configure the geographic location for storing data to comply with government regulations in different countries?
- What is their process and protocol for handling security breaches?
- If a breach occurs, what is their policy for notifying the cloud-based customer?

The legal landscape for cloud computing still contains many gray areas. Carefully note any differences in contractual obligations from provider to provider or from geography to geography. Make sure it is clear whether the responsibility for complying with country-specific laws and regulations rests with the provider, the system integrator, or your company.

Also, clarify what may happen if the provider gets into financial or legal trouble. What assurances will you have that your operations will not be affected, and what recourse will you have if they are? If the provider's minimum obligations do not satisfy your needs, try to negotiate for a better arrangement.

There are many, including Internet co-creator Vint Cerf,[10] who believe cloud providers will, in the long run, maintain environments that are more secure than the environments many organizations maintain themselves, because of increased emphasis, expertise, and automation around security. In the meantime, make sure your questions are thorough.

Enterprise Fit

Not all cloud providers are a good fit for large companies. You need to ensure the provider can meet the needs of a corporation of your size. Ask the following:

- Do they have a track record of reliable operations? Do they have SLAs that meet enterprise-level requirements—for example, "three-9s"

[10] "Vint Cerf: Very Concerned About Hacking Incidents." WSJ Video. http://online.wsj.com/video/vint-cerf-very-concerned-about-hacking-incidents/36F64FF9-FCDA-454C-9146-19848ED7AA8C.html

(99.9 percent) or greater service availability? Are penalties or service credits built into the SLA to address any shortcomings?
- Do they offer specialized support services or technical account managers to address the needs of customers with large user bases? How do they work with customers to develop an operational responsibility matrix?
- Can they tell you the I/O speed of storage? If so, can they explain how it impacts cloud performance?
- Which administrative and operational tools do they offer? Do they allow the enterprise to capture metrics in sufficient detail?
- How many global data centers do they have? Do they offer content delivery networks? What measures have they taken to address latency issues for geographically distributed users?

Future Roadmap

Many cloud providers are working to fill gaps in their offerings. SaaS providers, for example, are creating new tools to help migrate user accounts and data. Administrative tools and APIs continue to evolve. Some providers are in the process of pursuing certifications and attestations to meet security and compliance requirements. It is helpful to explore their roadmap for new features with prospective cloud providers:

- Does the provider seem open to sharing their roadmap?
- How quickly do they plan to include features that you need? Might the provider consider your requirements as they build new tools and features?
- Does the provider have plans for additional APIs, developer toolkits, or component libraries?
- Which migration tools are in the works? Do the planned tools and features meet your middle- or long-term migration needs?

One way to validate the information that cloud providers have provided is to use them on a trial basis. Pick a low-risk, simple application and pilot it on more than one provider's platform. Doing so may still not get you an "apples-to-apples" comparison on price and value, but you will come away knowing which providers represented their services and support accurately. You will also gain a better understanding of which one would make the best long-term partner.

Upgrade the Organization

Cloud adoption done well refocuses IT from buying and supporting infrastructure to managing the company's portfolio of technology investments and partnering more closely in business innovation. The CIO becomes the guardian of business data, the voice of the business unit with vendors, and the architect for end-to-end systems that extend far beyond the company's private network. You need to be prepared for the cascading effects these changes will have across your company.

Cloud Training

Your cloud readiness assessment should reveal where engineers and operations personnel have gaps in knowledge and understanding about the cloud. Enlisting managers and stakeholders in a company-wide cloud awareness campaign that includes training is vital.

Three categories of training warrant investment, especially for enterprises wanting to adopt the cloud within the next three to five years.

- **Technical training** A two-day technical course can cover coding practices for engineering and management tools for operations, as well as architecture and information security.
- **Manager training** Program and project managers need to understand the benefits of the cloud, the basics of cloud computing, and the tools/techniques to identify the best candidates for migration. A one-day course is often sufficient.
- **Business stakeholder training** The goal for this training is to evangelize cloud computing to a select group of senior business partners within the organization. Generally, a half-day course is ample.

Microsoft IT spent roughly 70 percent of its time and resources on technical training, 20 percent on management training, and 10 percent on business stakeholder training. This ratio may vary for organizations that outsource the majority of their engineering and operations work. With the appropriate investment, most enterprises should be able to train their entire organization within two years.

To supplement cloud training, we have encouraged knowledge sharing through programs such as Windows Azure Sandbox and The Garage Science Fair (described in the Epilogue). In our experience, sharing lessons learned (for example, through brown bag sessions, demos, and webcasts) calls attention to cloud migration activities, generating internal buzz and offering concrete signs of progress.

Cloud Governance

As you transform your organization to embrace cloud computing, governance will be essential. You need policies in place to guide resource allocation, funding, and project prioritization.

In Chapter 2 we suggested creating a cross-functional team of managers to steer the long-term cloud adoption process. Microsoft IT's Cloud Adoption Steering Committee provided guidance to help make critical decisions and assess risks, prioritize investments, and facilitate communication to the rest of the organization. The structure of the committee Microsoft IT used is shown in the following illustration:

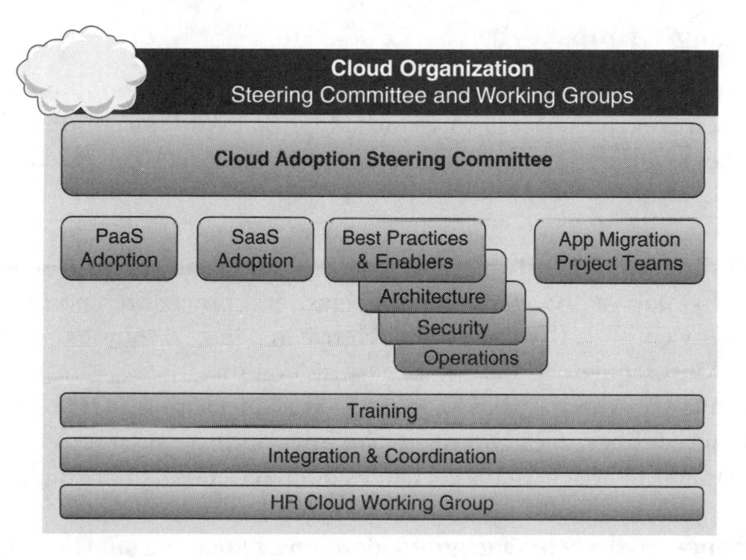

The CIO plays the critical role of removing barriers and eliminating decision gridlock, and he or she needs the support and participation of leaders from departments outside IT, particularly since changes to budget, governance, and technology implementation processes will affect them. We suggest you invite the following mix of senior managers to serve in your cloud steering committee:

- **Information security sponsor/executive** The person in charge of information security is responsible for understanding the implications of adoption from a security and privacy perspective and ensuring readiness.

- **HR sponsor/executive** It is important to prepare for organizational impact, including potential reductions in the operations organization and redefinition of roles. The HR sponsor leads this effort.
- **Finance sponsor/executive** The CFO, or the person responsible for IT finance, must ensure proper funding for your cloud strategy and will hold IT accountable for meeting ROI standards.
- **Engineering and operations sponsors/executives** These individuals drive core engineering, operational planning, and readiness.
- **Enterprise architecture group** This group may be its own department or a virtual team and will ensure adherence to architecture standards as adoption progresses. They already understand the current ecosystem and topology of IT applications and systems, so they can recommend where to focus efforts and identify potential stumbling blocks.

Working Groups

The steering committee will face many decisions about organizing and focusing the process of cloud adoption. Working groups aligned with key committee roles can be valuable resources for research and analysis.

- **Information security** A group of security subject matter experts (SMEs) can define standards, policies, and procedures pertaining to security controls (for example, "defense in depth"), coding or architecture, and regulatory and privacy considerations.
- **Human resources** Based on real-world experience, this working group redefines roles and responsibilities and suggests potential organizational changes, such as head count reduction that might result from shifting operations to the cloud.
- **Finance** This working group develops budgeting and billing processes to ensure predictable and consistent financials. It also defines ROI targets and success metrics.
- **Technical readiness** Architectural, engineering, and operational staff analyze patterns, practices, and readiness. They can promote consistency across the organization and identify opportunities for simplification, such as shared services, as described in Chapter 2.

New Roles and Responsibilities

Cloud adoption introduces a level of automation that can eliminate the need for many design, configuration, and hardware procurement tasks, ultimately reducing or eliminating IT roles. With fewer infrastructure management obligations, the engineering and operations staff will have more time to spend on higher value-add areas.

The CIO will need to work with HR, IT, and other business managers to determine how cloud adoption will change the organization. Knowledge transfer and cross-functional training will, for a time, become a dominant concern.

- **Reduce** Acknowledge that some roles will become redundant as various ongoing operational responsibilities shift to cloud providers or simply disappear. HR and IT management should work together to clarify staff reduction goals, strategies, and costs.
- **Retain and reward** Part of your challenge might be retaining workers with valuable skills. Seek ways to reward staff for considering a shift in responsibilities or a new position within the company. Executive sponsorship can encourage this by aligning employee evaluations to cloud initiatives, where possible.
- **Resource** Find the right providers, vendors, partners, and consultants to handle tasks you prefer to outsource. It is important that you ensure that retained employees work well with them.

Successful organizational change boils down to strong leadership. Understanding the language of business and IT's shifting role in supporting the business will be crucial for employees seeking advancement.

DevOps

Cloud computing will blur the boundaries between engineering and operations. Software developers will need to think a little more like system administrators and operations staff, who, in turn, will need to think more like developers and testers. The skill sets of operational personnel will generally increase as fewer, more technically skilled staff remain. This new landscape is fertile ground for DevOps.

In a DevOps model, software developers have a better understanding of the operational patterns and practices that enable high availability and performance. While operations personnel are not expected to have the same level of development skills as programmers, they must nevertheless have a basic understanding of the technologies programmers use to build services. Familiarity with cloud APIs will help them become better at automating administrative tasks.

A DevOps team shares joint responsibility for problem resolution. Development, quality assurance, and operations may even become a single unified team. The DevOps model facilitates a move from waterfall software development to more agile iterative approaches, allowing for faster response to user demands that require scale and new application functionality. A summary of the key differences between traditional and DevOps models are outlined in the following illustration:

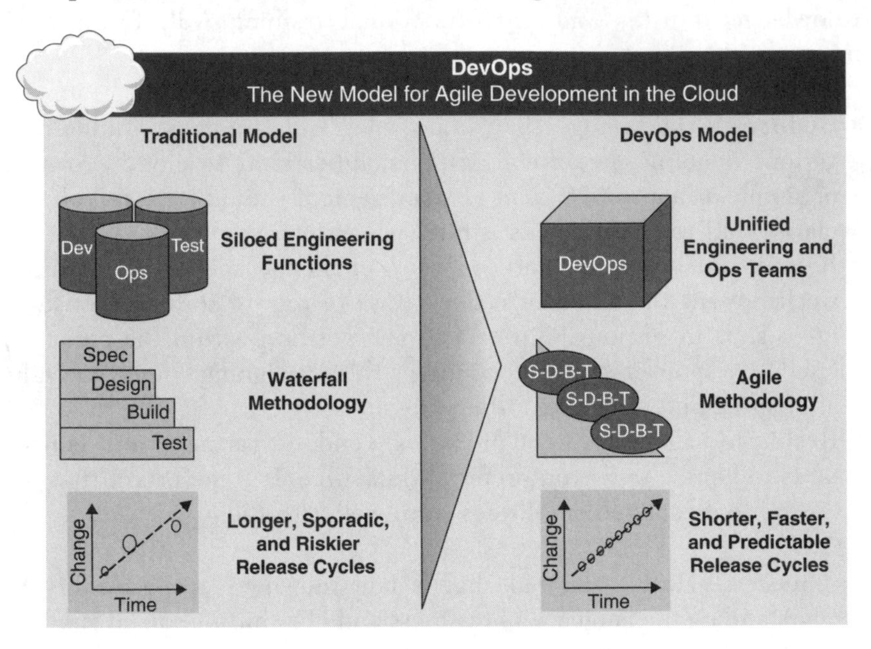

Web 2.0 companies such as Netflix and Flickr have written about their experiences using the DevOps model. In a presentation at Velocity 2009 entitled "10+ Deploys per Day: Dev and Ops Cooperation at Flickr," John Allspaw and Paul Hammond described how Flickr teams applied DevOps concepts to roll out as many as ten deployments in a day. They automated the deployment of infrastructure, created a one-step build and deploy process for shipping releases, and used online collaboration to coordinate issue resolution during releases.

Adrian Cockcroft's April 2011 presentation about Netflix's full migration of its website to public cloud services, entitled "Moving Your Organization to Public Cloud," drew many of the same conclusions about DevOps as Allspaw and Hammond did. Developers remain the owners of code running in production environments. Operations work shifts to writing code and creating tools that automate processes. Both roles have a part to play in collecting metrics. A flatter and more collaborative IT organization is necessary to accomplish all of this.

Most enterprise IT groups already have release management processes in place. DevOps can reduce development cycles from weeks or months to days or weeks, which means project managers or release coordinators will see a corresponding shift in their duties. Releasing smaller components more often lessens the risk of failures, assuming rollbacks are easy.

We suggest you take a close look at agile software development methodologies, such as Scrum, if you have not already done so. Also consider changing job descriptions or performance review goals to encourage better collaboration among IT staff. For example, educational goals could include "Operations engineers demonstrate a working knowledge of detailed systems design," or "Software developers work one shift to support applications they built (per week, month, or quarter)."

Revamp Tools and Processes

With a steering committee and working groups in place, you are ready to tackle the task of analyzing your existing policies and processes. The following section summarizes changes to explore.

Cloud Policy

As your company's vision for cloud adoption crystallizes and migration planning begins in earnest, consider setting some guidelines for cloud migrations around the following:

- When business units may select SaaS, and how to involve IT in the process
- Which types of business information may or may not be moved to cloud storage
- Minimum standards for securing information at rest and in transit
- Infrastructure and application architecture standards or design patterns to follow
- How to think about identity and account management in the cloud

Your information security working group should suggest appropriate ways to tighten or loosen standards, policies, and procedures that enable cloud adoption to proceed without introducing unwarranted risks to the business.

If your organization does not already have a Chief Information Security Officer (CISO) role, consider creating the role or one like it. If a senior management role already fulfills this function, consider shifting it to report to the CIO or to be more directly linked to the CIO role, as cloud computing will increase the visibility of safeguarding corporate information.

Finance Process Changes

Because cloud providers own the servers and other fixed assets behind their services, outsourcing IT operations to them results in operational expenses (OPEX) for services rendered rather than capital expenditures (CAPEX) for equipment. This change has several ramifications for finance processes.

Traditionally, IT-related CAPEX planning has been for multiyear increments, whereas OPEX planning has been more of an annual exercise. Today, CIOs buy capacity in phases. They know how much each phase will cost and how long the purchased capacity will meet their needs, and they can budget accordingly. In the cloud, that type of planning is no longer relevant. CIOs will now need a multiyear OPEX plan, as they need to project how operational drivers, such as storage growth, will affect costs over time—something that will become easier to measure from month to month or quarter to quarter. Budgeting processes for hybrid environments will be more complex, as budgeting must plan for both on-premises data center CAPEX and cloud-related OPEX.

CIOs also need to understand how the speed and volume of changes in operational drivers, such as storage and bandwidth requirements, will determine how much their cloud provider charges. CIOs, to some degree, can throttle the rate of change in available capacity (that is, supply). However, they cannot control the volume of change required, because that is driven by business needs (that is, demand). They also cannot, of course, change the speed at which demand grows. CIOs will need to help their business partners understand how changes in volume will affect IT costs. They need the ability to track costs related to the rate of change separately from the cost of changes in volume.

Your finance working group can help determine what other impact might occur from shifting more of the IT budget from CAPEX to OPEX. It is a common practice, for example, to underwrite purchasing or supporting infrastructure components for one business unit through chargebacks to another unit. Furthermore, application-level chargeback models do not often line up to true costs; that is, some applications can subsidize others through bias in internal chargeback models. The move to variable costs, the necessity to pay only for the capacity actually reserved or used, and the ability to track costs cleanly on an application-by-application basis provide greater visibility into true operational costs. This might require finance and IT to make significant revisions to budgeting and chargeback models as "fluffing" the budget in one area to help cover the costs for another becomes unnecessary.

Key finance-related questions include the following:

- Is there a way for cloud migration to fund itself?
- How much can you invest in training or consulting to speed the process along?
- How close are you to the next major hardware refresh for your IT infrastructure? How much of that budget could be reallocated to cloud migration?
- Could a chargeback model for cloud-based services work effectively? How large a shift would this be, given the existing IT financial model in your company?

A budgeting factor to watch closely is that of expected versus actual usage. In some cases, an application moved to the cloud can experience an unforeseen increase in demand. Tighter coupling of use metrics to budget criteria can help IT determine whether it should allow a high-demand application to scale automatically.

We also recommend having these conversations with your CFO or finance counterparts. By partnering with your finance organization, you can ensure that IT and finance are in alignment with regard to these changes.

Development Process Changes

The ease and low cost of spinning up environments in the cloud, lower operational overhead, and the availability of tools and finished services put enterprises in a better position to increase the speed and level of innovation.

Establishing a framework for migrating or building applications with repeatable processes makes cloud-based development simpler and faster. The framework should include an end-to-end workflow that guides architecture design, security practices (such as code reviews), regulatory compliance, and other factors. It should also provide company policies for using the cloud, templates, and checklists for tracking project health and managing risks. Finally, because agility is a primary motivation for adopting cloud computing, the framework must be conducive to rapid application development. This might challenge some enterprises to shed processes that are traditionally bureaucratic.

Cloud Tools

The odds are that you will select a cloud provider that supports technologies familiar to your staff, in which case developers will already have access to tools that aid cloud-based application development. Many cloud providers offer specialized tools and kits to make developing applications easier for their services. For example, although its core programming languages and models are the same as for Windows Server, Windows Azure offers special SDKs that integrate with Visual Studio.

Enabling instrumentation, for example, for monitoring cloud services, can require different tools or approaches than it would on-premises. How an application hooks into cloud monitoring tools that your provider supports will vary depending on which provider and set of technologies you choose. Cloud training and pilots will help you identify which tools your teams will need.

Summary

- You can take a gradual, a balanced, or an aggressive approach to cloud adoption in terms of how fast you move, whether you centralize or decentralize labor, whether you perform migration in-house or use vendors, and whether you use a top-down or bottom-up style of management.
- Pilot migrations can help fill technical knowledge gaps, test whether expected benefits can be realized, and provide cost-savings data.
- Start with a couple of applications that have a small or medium level of demand with a comparable degree of complexity. Push the applications beyond their expected limits in the testing phase to understand the costs of running them in the cloud.
- Select a cloud provider based on the services it offers, how long it has been in business, the maturity of its business processes, the thoroughness of contracts and SLAs, and how clearly and completely its representatives answer your questions.
- Select a "true cloud provider" whose current and planned technologies fit your needs. Carefully analyze how much the applications in your portfolio might cost to run in the cloud based on the provider's pricing model. Understand how well the provider handles both technical and legal issues regarding security, and ensure their services meet the requirements of companies similar in size to yours.
- With the appropriate investment, most enterprises can train their entire organization within two years. Spend approximately 70 percent of time and resources on technical training, 20 percent on management training, and 10 percent on business stakeholder training.

- Cloud governance is important for putting policies in place to guide resource allocation, funding, and project prioritization. The combination of a steering committee and working groups can manage this process.
- The CIO will need to work with managers in HR, IT, and other business groups to determine how cloud adoption will change the organization—for example, if it will result in some reduction of the workforce or shifting of roles.
- Review standards, policies, and procedures. Understand how cloud computing might impact finance and development processes.
- In a DevOps model, software developers understand operational patterns and practices, and operations personnel understand the technologies programmers use to build services. A DevOps model facilitates moving from waterfall software development to a more agile iterative approach.

Chapter 4

Execute

Many enterprises struggle to manage heterogeneous environments that include legacy hardware and software. Inconsistencies in system configurations tend to proliferate, and long-term contracts for third-party solutions make it hard to switch vendors. Over time, IT gets mired in just keeping track of and maintaining all the individual applications. As a result, engineering and operations have less time to focus on finding new or better ways to provide the functionality that the business needs. Using cloud services to help solve these problems introduces the need to think differently about solution architecture, design, implementation, and operations.

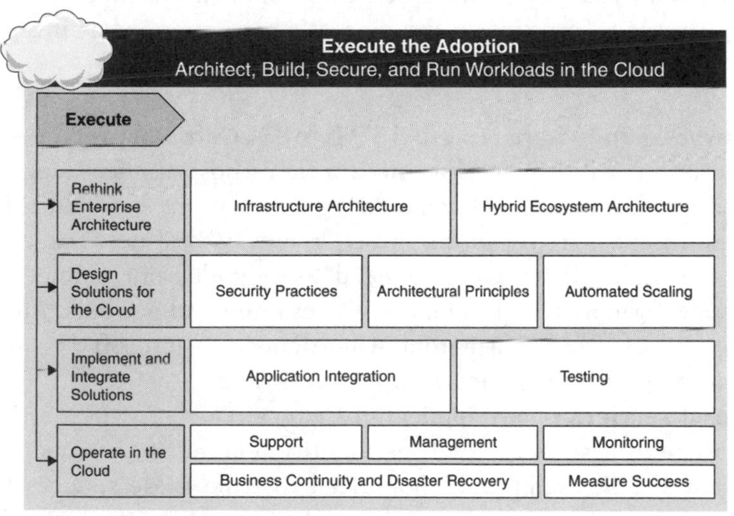

Rethink Enterprise Architecture

In the cloud, IT should not focus simply on managing a portfolio of individual applications that deliver multiple and perhaps complex functions for a single business unit's needs. Instead, by looking at the entire set of IT systems to see where information, service, and process requirements converge, IT can achieve greater efficiencies, cost savings, and increased agility.

Infrastructure Architecture

Although developers no longer need to wait for new servers when scaling out to accommodate a spike in demand, they still need to pay attention to how many servers they use. Scaling out requires adherence to design principles similar to those of the client/server model—use service-oriented designs, distribute application components to the appropriate layers, and architect an appropriate data schema. To take full advantage of scalability, application logic needs to be modular and loosely coupled rather than monolithic, as it is in some legacy applications.

On-Premises Optimizations

Enterprise on-premises systems designed for high availability and redundancy may already apply some architecture principles relevant to cloud computing. It is important to examine two areas of on-premises dependencies that arise with cloud migration: network bandwidth and shared services. Investing in these areas is as important as investing in tools and applications.

- **Network bandwidth** Internal LAN/WAN traffic between users and applications will become Internet traffic if those applications move to a public cloud. Although refactoring applications can address some latency issues, if the on-premises "roadway" for network traffic is causing a slowdown, you will need to upgrade your connectivity to meet performance requirements. For example, after we identified our web proxy servers as a potential bottleneck, Microsoft IT upgraded them to optimize Internet network bandwidth.
- **Shared services** Your applications may already rely on some shared infrastructure services, such as identity federation systems. As with the bandwidth example, IT may need to scale these services to support additional load from cloud-based applications that now depend on them. Furthermore, enterprises with shared lab environments or VM on-demand services may benefit from hosting these services in the cloud.

The following illustration summarizes some of the areas of potential impact to on-premises infrastructure.

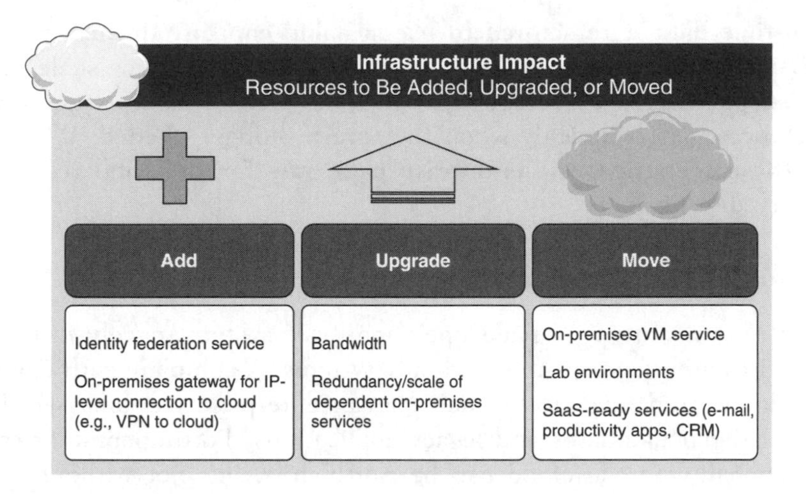

As you analyze your network topology, you need to review whether you have enough redundancy to prevent single points of failure in the corporate network. Because users inside the firewall lose access to applications on a public cloud if Internet connectivity is lost, you should add redundancy to your environment where there is none or not enough. For example, take a look at identity management and any other shared services currently hosted on-premises so that they do not become bottlenecks or single points of failure.

Although investment in some infrastructure components might still be necessary, enterprises can slow down or even stop procuring physical servers with a major migration to cloud services. One way to offset the financial impact of any remaining investments is to flag applications running on aging servers as candidates for cloud migration rather than proceeding with server replacements. This same idea applies to moving infrastructure services such as e-mail or collaboration to the cloud.

Impact of Cloud Infrastructure Services

Some cloud platforms provide finished infrastructure services, such as caching, that developers can simply plug into and use to save time and effort. Using cloud caching is also a great way to help prevent latency issues. Similar services for identity management, enterprise service bus, workflow, and messaging integration can help reduce infrastructure-related expenses.

An increasing number of cloud platforms simplify creation and configuration of application scale units by offering auto-scaling as a core service. Batch processing applications that could once find enough capacity to run only in the middle of the night can offer real-time data if refactored to use scalable capacity during the day. I/O-intensive applications can automatically spin up new scale units to support periods of high demand and then decommission those instances just as quickly when they are no longer needed. With any of these scenarios, the enterprise pays only for the total resources reserved or used.

Hybrid Ecosystem Architecture

Few, if any, enterprise-scale operations will switch entirely from on-premises architectures to cloud-only systems. A company with enough employees and revenue to qualify as an enterprise has amassed data in relational databases and legacy applications. Porting some of their functionality to the cloud can be worthwhile, but not without some refactoring.

Two high-level scenarios require a hybrid application ecosystem:

- **Applications move to the cloud while some dependent services remain on-premises** For example, application X moves to the cloud. It still communicates with application Y and uses an e-mail service called application Z, but neither application Y nor application Z move to the cloud. This scenario will exist for most enterprises.
- **An application's architecture is intentionally split across premises** For example, the presentation and business logic layers move to the cloud while the database remains on-premises. This scenario is often a choice; there might be interim scenarios in which certain application components initially stay on-premises.

Companies that collect, manage, and use highly sensitive customer information will take longer to test the security and reliability of cloud services before deciding whether to move all data into cloud storage. Some will keep data on-premises. They might opt to use cloud services only to enable application access or present content to end users. Additional hybrid scenarios include cloud bursting, backup, disaster recovery, and failover.

Deploying applications as hybrid architectures increases the likelihood of latency-related issues. Application developers and operations personnel may not currently focus heavily on latency optimization. This is because latency interferes less with application performance when servers are on-premises and communicate over a local area network (LAN), and when all components are co-located within the same data center.

In hybrid scenarios, issues that formerly did not matter take on new importance. For example, "chattier" applications, or those with heavy payloads across hybrid components, have a higher probability of end-user performance issues. Geographic separation between application components and users across the Internet magnifies latency issues.

Imagine an on-premises application designed with no concern for the number of SQL round trips needed to process transactions because the web server and SQL server are in the same data center inside the company's LAN, where latency is minimal. Moving the UI layer of this application to a public cloud while keeping the database on-premises will degrade performance due to the Internet's latency, and "chatter" will increase the bill from the cloud provider.

New security concerns also emerge with hybrid architectures. For example, cross-premises connections must be secured since they communicate over the public Internet. Use of Secure Sockets Layer (SSL) and certificate-based authentication should be a standard design practice. Some integration services available through cloud providers include measures such as IP security or encryption to help with security.

A hybrid architecture also presents some manageability and support challenges. Management tools will need extensions to provide a single view of system health across cloud-based and on-premises components. Analysis procedures are necessary so that support can trace whether the root cause of an issue is in the cloud or on-premises.

Design Solutions for the Cloud

Although most basic coding techniques remain the same, developing for the cloud is different in key ways that involve security, testing, and application architecture.

Security Practices

Security and compliance concerns, while never far from mind, take on heightened importance, because cloud-based applications live outside the corporate firewall and have a larger attack surface. News reports of sophisticated malicious attempts to obtain identities or sensitive data might make organizations skittish about adopting cloud services. Security concerns heighten when a growing assortment of less secure devices, such as mobile phones, access cloud applications.

Security is an extensive, in-depth topic that is both art and science. Here, we will focus on issues that are particularly relevant to the cloud.

The following table summarizes key security questions you will need to address.

Area	Questions
Policies and standards	Which of your policies and standards will need to change in a cloud environment? How will you enforce your policies and standards in a cloud infrastructure that a third party owns and manages? Does the cloud environment you have selected follow existing standards/frameworks, such as International Organization for Standardization (ISO) standards and Control Objectives for Information and related Technology (COBIT), for security controls and governance?
Design	How will you secure applications and data in the cloud? Is your Identity Access Management architecture appropriate for the cloud?
Development	How should you update your design review process to cover cloud-specific security requirements? What code review areas should you add? What test cases? How will you secure development and test environments in the cloud?
Operations	How do you secure your network as it extends into the cloud? How do you ensure that your provider's cloud management infrastructure is secure? How will you monitor security in the cloud? For a hybrid environment?
Incident response	How will you update your security incident response protocol for a cloud environment? Will your cloud provider work with you to manage security incidents? What SLA will it provide?

As discussed earlier, selection criteria for an Infrastructure as a Service (IaaS) or Platform as a Service (PaaS) provider should be how it secures resources and whether it will be possible to meet your current security standards and enforce your existing policies. Some providers may offer turnkey options for building authentication and authorization into the cloud-based application.

Although keeping information safe is a responsibility shared across cloud providers, enterprise IT, and the end user, ensuring security begins with sound engineering practices. IT and software engineering departments can use standard security processes and controls to safeguard corporate assets in the cloud. For example, you can use SSL for transferring sensitive data from a server to a browser or to another server.

Encrypting files helps to protect data at rest. Cloud providers make a variety of encryption technologies available, some native to their offering and others through the operating systems they support. For example, Windows-based virtual machines running on Amazon EC2 can encrypt files using the Encrypting File System (EFS) feature built into Windows. Similar mechanisms may exist or can be custom-implemented for cloud table storage or binary large objects (BLOBs).

Using encryption introduces another potential security challenge—that of managing keys. Understanding how encryption solutions manage keys will help you in establishing procedures to prevent their exposure.

Many cloud providers use some form of developer credentials, often in the form of access keys and certificates, to permit access to their APIs. Similar authentication credentials might be required to connect to back-ends such as SQL servers. These keys and passwords should be encrypted, preferably in a secure store. When communicating with back-end services, keys and passwords should be decrypted only temporarily and in memory only.

We have mentioned the importance of identity management. Granting the least privileges necessary remains an important security practice. Other security controls include policies around resetting passwords on a routine basis, limiting who has which cloud passwords, and requiring dual-factor authentication.

Finally, consider ways to secure the "application perimeter." Some cloud providers offer firewalls. With IaaS, administrators can even use software-based firewalls available through the operating systems of virtual machine instances. They can invoke similar functionality in PaaS. Standard IP filtering techniques can restrict incoming traffic based on security policies and network access control lists (ACLs).

Code Reviews

Technology news is replete with headlines about web services or online accounts that have been hacked. Although many cyber-attacks use elaborate social engineering tactics to gain access, others can be traced to failure by companies to take some of the most basic measures to protect against known exploits. Talk to the team that creates and maintains your corporate website. They will have knowledge and experience on how to reduce the chances that malicious attackers will hack your cloud-based services.

Having IP access rules in place to restrict public cloud-based applications is a good start, but securing the application directly is even better. Components stored or run in cloud platforms will need to meet a higher security standard. To prevent any security holes or issues from reaching a public cloud, you can enforce a policy requiring applications to pass a security code review before they are released to production. Code should always be checked for vulnerabilities such as cross-site scripting or holes that would allow a SQL injection attack to succeed. Have your security experts put together a comprehensive checklist for developers, and ensure that they follow good security design practices.

When attacks against Microsoft software increased, the company pioneered the Security Development Lifecycle (SDL). Its use has been mandatory for all Microsoft engineering teams since 2004, and it has significantly reduced incidents traced to security holes in Microsoft software. Information on how to use the SDL is publicly available at http://www.microsoft.com/security/sdl/default.aspx.

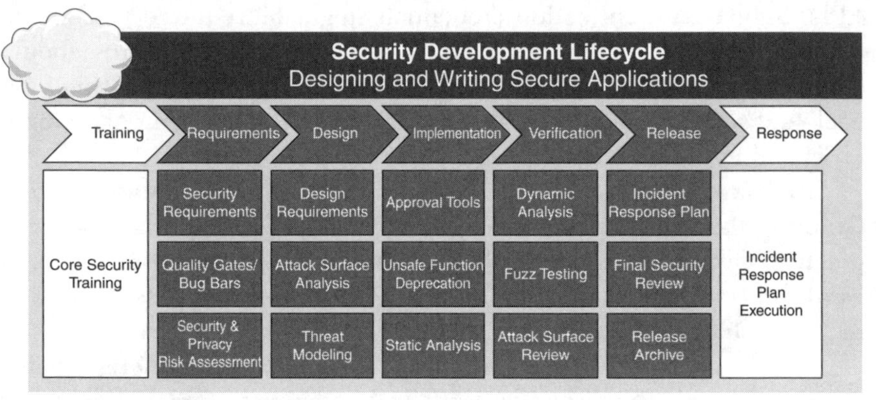

Attack and Penetration Testing

You will want to verify that particularly critical applications are secure in production. One method is to have a separate team attempt to break into the application or to perform mild forms of denial-of-service attacks. Be sure to follow policies and processes of cloud providers that facilitate this kind of testing so that you do not cause problems for other cloud tenants. (In other words, be careful not to violate your terms of service.)

Traditionally, attackers will either attack servers and applications on corporate premises or use a corporate user as an entry point. They might now have a new way to uncover corporate data if they can find a weakness in the cloud. Although cloud providers have safeguards in place, some level of risk is always present. Whether a third party conducts the test or your company does, it is important that testing include the following basic attacker roles:

- **External users** Unauthenticated users attacking from the Internet

- **Insiders** Authenticated application users attacking from the Internet or corporate network
- **Tenant neighbors** Unauthenticated users attacking from another cloud provider customer

Your list of high-level test cases can vary from application to application depending on the architecture and the sensitivity of the business information accessed. Common testing scenarios include the following:

- Denial-of-service attacks
- Errors and exception management
- Session management vulnerabilities
- Data security holes, such as SQL injection attacks, file system traversal and cross-site scripting, manipulation of parameters, weak passwords, and lack of encryption (in transit or at rest)

Monitoring and Logging

To monitor security for cloud-based applications, IT staff needs access to an appropriate level of logging capabilities. Although most cloud providers perform general monitoring on their infrastructures, responsibility for ensuring that there is no unauthorized access to an application rests with the enterprise.

Implementing tools for easy review of audit logs is desirable, particularly for higher sensitivity applications. It is a good idea to build functionality, such as a shared service plug-in, to track failed login attempts, IP addresses of connections, and administrator actions.

Ongoing Refinements

The cloud is a dynamic hosting environment in which technologies and business models continue to evolve, and security is an extremely dynamic field. Moreover, enterprise CIOs must adhere to continually updated regulatory requirements related to delivering services globally online, including those issued by governments, from legal rulings, and from industry standards. These continuous changes are a challenge that corporations must address through an effective and equally dynamic security program.

Reviewing policy and procedures at minimum on an annual basis will help ensure that the controls, which are used to mitigate risk, remain relevant. As mentioned, many companies have created a CISO or a similar role to give such activities the priority they deserve.

Architectural Principles

Moving applications and data out of the corporate data center does not eliminate the risk of hardware failures, unexpected demand for an application, or unforeseen problems that arise in production. Designed well, however, a service running in the cloud should be more scalable and fault-tolerant, and it should perform better than an on-premises solution.

Virtualization and cloud fabric technologies, as used by cloud providers, make it possible to scale out to a theoretically unlimited capacity. This means that application architecture and the level of automation, not physical capacity, constrain scalability. In this section, we introduce several design principles that application engineers and operations personnel need to understand to architect a highly scalable and reliable application for the cloud.

Resiliency

A properly designed application will not go down just because something happens to a single scale unit. A poorly designed application, in contrast, may experience performance problems, data loss, or an outage when a single component fails. This is why cloud-centric software engineers cultivate a certain level of pessimism. By thinking of all the worst-case scenarios, they can design applications that are fault-tolerant and resilient when something goes wrong.

Monolithic software design, in which the presentation layer and functional logic are tightly integrated into one application component, may not scale effectively or handle failure gracefully. To optimize an application for the cloud, developers need to eliminate tight dependencies and break the business logic and tasks into loosely coupled modular components so that they can function independently. Ideally, application functionality will consist of autonomous roles that function regardless of the state of other application components. To minimize enterprise complexity, developers should also leverage reusable services where possible.

We talked about the Microsoft online auction tool in Chapter 3. One way to design such an application would be to split it into three components, as each service has a different demand pattern and is relatively asynchronous from the others: a UI layer responsible for presenting information to the user, an image resizer, and a business logic component that applies the bidding rules and makes the appropriate database updates. At the start of the auction, a lot of image resizing occurs as people upload pictures of items they add to the catalog. Toward the end of the auction, as people try to outbid each other, the bidding engine is in higher demand. Each component adds scale units as needed based on system load. Furthermore if, for example, the image resizer component fails, the entire functionality of the tool is not lost. This architecture and scenario is illustrated in the following diagram:

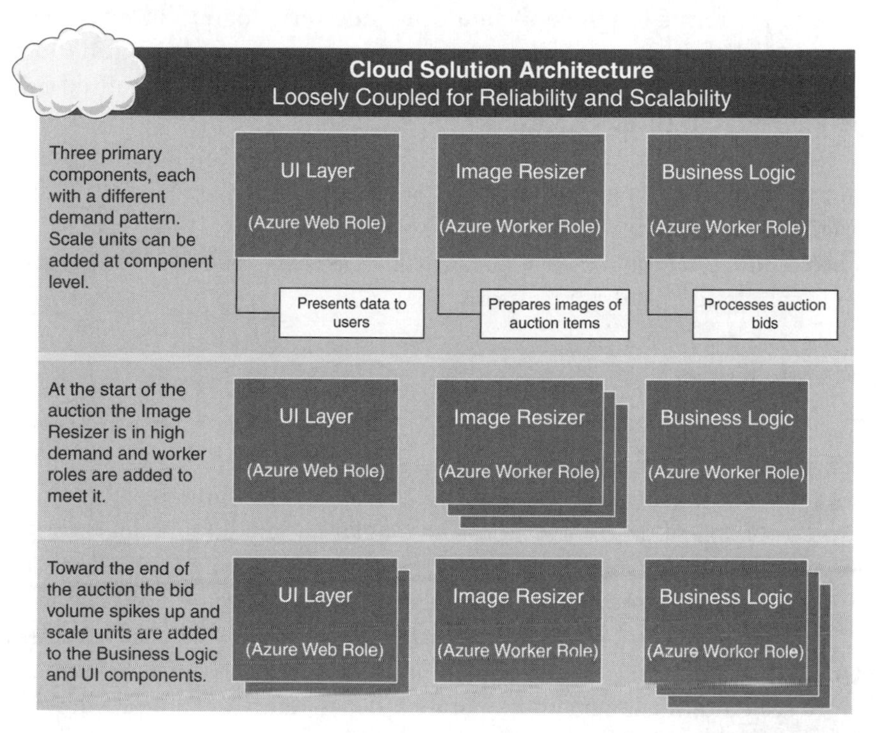

Pessimism aside, the redundancy and automation built into cloud models make cloud services more reliable, in general. Often, cloud providers have multiple "availability zones" in which they segment network infrastructure, hardware, and even power from one another. Operating multiple scale units of a single application across these zones can further reduce risk; some providers require this before they will guarantee a higher SLA. Therefore, the real questions when considering failure are

- What happens if an instance of an application is abruptly rebooted, goes down, or is moved?
- How will IT know the failure occurred?
- What application functionality, if any, will still be available?
- Which steps will be required to recover data and functionality for users?

Removing unnecessary dependencies makes applications more stable. If a service upon which the application relies for one usage scenario goes down, other application scenarios should remain available.

For the back-end, because some cloud providers might throttle requests or terminate long-running queries on SQL PaaS and other storage platforms, engineers should include retry logic. For example, a component that requests data from another source could include logic that asks for the data a specified number of times within a specified time period before it throws an exception.

For the occasional reboot of a cloud instance, application design should include a persistent cache so that another scale unit or the original instance that reboots can recover transactions. Using persistent state requires taking a closer look at statelessness—another design principle for cloud-based applications.

Statelessness

Designing for statelessness is crucial for scalability and fault tolerance in the cloud. Whether an outage is unexpected or planned (as with an operating system update), as one scale unit goes down, another picks up the work. An application user should not notice that anything happened. It is important to deploy more than one scale unit for each critical cloud service, if not for scaling purposes, then simply for redundancy and availability.

Cloud providers generally necessitate that applications be stateless. During a single session, users of an application can interact with one or more scale unit instances that operate independently in what is known as "stateless load balancing" or "lack of session affinity." Developers should not hold application or session state in the working memory of a scale unit, because there is no guarantee the user will exclusively interact with that particular scale unit. Therefore, without stateless design, many applications will not be able to scale out properly in the cloud. Most cloud providers offer persistent storage to address this issue, allowing the application to store session state in a way that any scale unit can retrieve.

Parallelization

Taking advantage of parallelization and multithreaded application design improves performance and is a core cloud design principle. Load balancing and other services inherent in cloud platforms can help distribute load with relative ease. With low-cost rapid provisioning in the cloud, scale units are available on demand for parallel processing within a few API calls and are decommissioned just as easily.

Massive parallelization can also be used for high-performance computing scenarios, such as those for real-time enterprise data analytics. Many cloud providers directly or indirectly support frameworks that enable splitting up massive tasks for parallel processing. For example, Microsoft partnered with the University of Washington to demonstrate the power of Windows Azure for performing scientific research. The result was 2.5 million points of calculation performed by the equivalent of 2000 servers in less than one week,[11] a computing job that otherwise might have taken months.

Latency

Software engineers can apply the following general design principles to reduce the potential that network latency will interfere with availability and performance:

- Use caching, especially for data retrieved from higher latency systems, as would be the case with cross-premises systems.
- Reduce chattiness and/or payloads between components, especially when cross-premises integration is involved.
- Geo-distribute and replicate content globally. As mentioned, enabling the content delivery network in Windows Azure, for example, allows end users to receive BLOB storage content from the closest geographical location.

Automated Scaling

Numerous cloud providers, or their platform partners, enable auto-scaling through relatively simple configuration criteria. For instance, where this capability is not available, or if additional flexibility is desired, engineers can often poll existing monitoring APIs and use service-management APIs to build self-scaling capabilities into their applications. For example, consider utilization-based logic that automatically adds an application instance when traffic randomly spikes or reaches certain CPU consumption thresholds. The same routine might listen for messages, instructing instances to shut down once demand has fallen to more typical levels.

Some logic might be finance-based. For example, developers can add cost control logic to prevent noncritical applications from auto-scaling under specified conditions or to trigger alerts in case of usage spikes.

---

[11]"Scientists Unfolding Protein Mystery, Fighting Disease with Windows Azure." Microsoft. http://www.microsoft.com/presspass/features/2011/jun11/06-14proteinfolding.mspx

Although terminology and specifics vary, the following illustration provides the steps that typically occur inside cloud platforms to scale applications.

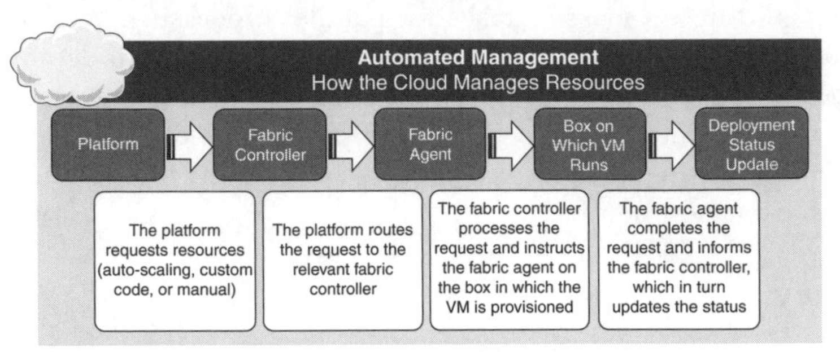

Scaling of data is as important as application scaling, and once again it is a matter of proper design. Rethinking the architecture of an application's data layer for use in the cloud, while potentially cumbersome, can also lead to performance and availability improvements. For example, if no cloud data storage service offers a solution large enough to contain the data in an existing database, consider breaking the dataset into partitions and storing it across multiple instances. This practice, known as "sharding," has become standard for many cloud platforms and is built into several, including SQL Azure. Even if this is not necessary initially, it might become so over time as data requirements grow.

Implement and Integrate Solutions

As discussed in Chapter 2, when making it a priority to build new applications as cloud-based solutions, an enterprise can reduce its total cost of ownership. A cloud-based solution incorporates statelessness, loosely coupled components, cloud data storage, and possibly finished services.

Leading cloud providers support many programming languages commonly used in enterprises, such as .NET languages, Java, and PHP. Cloud-based versions of standard programming languages are compatible with tools used on-premises today (for example, Microsoft SQL Server Management Studio, Microsoft Visual Studio, and so on), although software engineers may need to install SDKs to support cloud-based deployment scenarios. We anticipate that a similar range of cloud-tailored development environments, packaging and deployment tools, data access mechanisms, security services, and APIs will become as available for the cloud as they are for on-premises development.

Most cloud providers ensure that software engineers can write code either within the cloud environment or their local IT environment.

Some even offer tools that simulate cloud compute, scaling, or storage services. Although these tools let engineers test an application locally, they should still fully test and validate the application in the cloud to ensure that the solution works as expected. As the complexity and pace of change on cloud platforms might exceed that of on-premises cloud simulation tools, full testing in the cloud is essential.

Setting up environments for building, testing, and staging applications is as simple as creating scale units. There is no notion of separate "test" and "production" clouds. Instead, developers can use separate instances, which they define for different purposes, within the same cloud.

In some application migration scenarios, debugging applications can require as much work as developing them. We expect new capabilities will emerge to make debugging in the cloud easier.

Application Integration

Integrating legacy applications with cloud services raises several issues. One is determining how to connect services to each other across firewall boundaries. Another is identity management. The following illustration provides an overview of some common integration scenarios and the technology mechanisms involved.

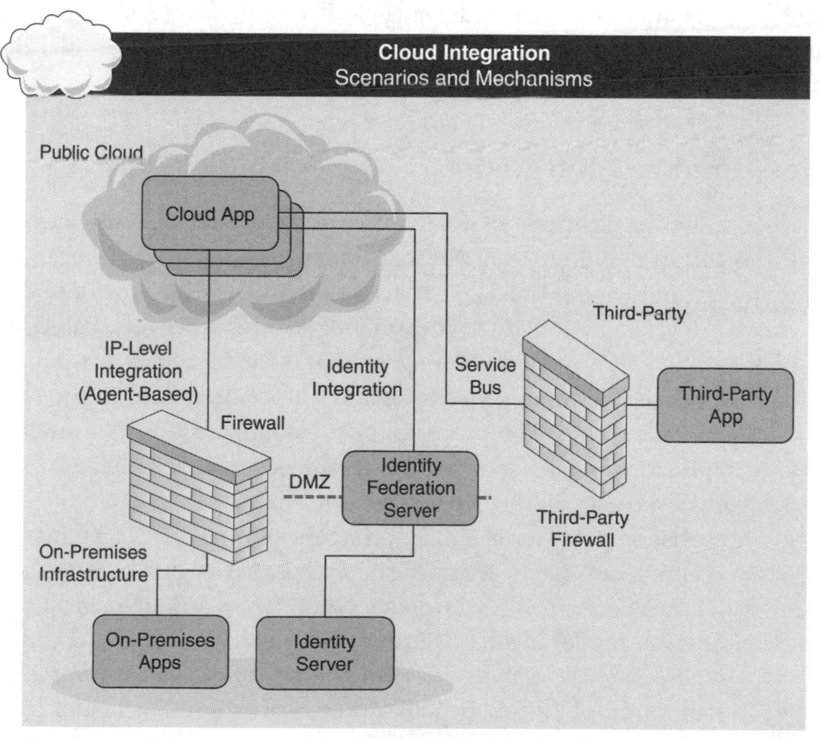

Identity Management

Enabling users, applications, or services to authenticate to cloud-based services requires identity integration to support the seamless use of corporate credentials and single sign-on for users. Companies that currently centralize authorization might be able to apply the same mechanisms to the cloud. Some cloud providers offer both authentication and authorization services via a federation or claims identity provider. Active Directory Federation Services is one example of an authentication service that allows seamless use of preexisting corporate credentials with cloud-based applications. This allows users to access applications from within the corporate network or over a virtual private network (VPN) connection without having to provide their credentials multiple times. Applications can also be accessible by users with corporate credentials over the Internet on public clouds, if desired.

Identity management services provide a trusted layer between the corporation's identity provider (such as Active Directory) and the cloud-based application. This identity layer transforms the user's credentials and claims (for example, attributes such as user name, job title, group, country, and so on) into a common token format that the cloud-based application can understand. The federated identity provider can also transform claims between different identity providers, allowing easy integration with other enterprises and even with consumer identities such as Facebook, Windows Live ID, or Google Account.

Cross-Premises Integration

There are two basic methods for connecting on-premises services with those hosted in cloud environments: use an IP connectivity layer or take advantage of messaging finished services that your cloud provider offers.

For IP-level connectivity, some providers offer an agent-based and/or a VPN-style gateway model. An agent-based model allows for point-to-point connectivity between services hosted on-premises and in the cloud. Installing an agent on the on-premises host establishes a VPN tunnel to a specific application in the cloud. Although the cost, speed, and ease of this model works for early trials, since it is decentralized, it does not scale easily in an enterprise setting (for example, an agent often needs to be installed on each on-premises server that will be integrated with cloud services). Using it can raise concerns about policy compliance and manageability.

The gateway model involves setting up a dedicated proxy to connect network segments or selected servers in the on-premises environment to nodes in the cloud platform. Because there is no need to install agents on each on-premises machine, this approach scales better than the agent-based approach. It also enables central management and monitoring of integration scenarios. For these reasons, enterprises generally prefer the gateway model for integration even though the start-up costs are higher.

Messaging or service bus finished service platforms allow traffic to pass through enterprise firewalls via a publicly accessible endpoint. These services provide additional capabilities such as multicast messaging, workflow, and durable storage that do more than just send data back and forth. Messaging capabilities can allow integration between partners without requiring integration at the IP level. Integration at a higher level in the cloud stack keeps entities more separate; this is an advantage when connecting with a third party whose security might not be up to your standards.

Multicast messaging is useful when an application needs to send a message to multiple subscribers. An example might be a "reverse auction" application in the cloud that asks for bids in response to a request for proposal (RFP). The RFP need only be published to the cloud's intermediary server, which would then automatically route it to vendors who subscribe to that message bus instance.

Adjustments in the application might be necessary to allow on-premises and cloud-hosted components to connect with one another. Using an IP-connectivity solution often requires less application rework than using finished services solutions such as a service bus.

Data Integration

Data as a Service (DaaS) solutions can use standardized data protocols, such as Open Data (OData), to share data between applications. Using the OData standard frees the application developer from writing custom data contracts between web services, which in turn makes it easier to integrate with any other service that uses the same standard. OData builds on other existing web technologies such as HTTP, XML, and JSON. Standards around web service contracts, as OData provides, also help break silos that form when legacy web services follow different design practices and technologies.

As data grows exponentially and the number of applications that need to access it grows over time, the cloud can serve as a convenient hub for data storage and integration. An enterprise can build a DaaS offering for internal or external data consumption, treating the cloud as the data hub and applications as the spokes. The cloud is ideal for large, central data stores because it can scale to accommodate growth in both database size and usage.

Testing

The following list summarizes several testing scenarios to perform on cloud solutions before moving them into production:

- **Mimic failure** Although high availability and redundancy are usually built into cloud services and backed by SLA guarantees, specific scale units can experience occasional "blips." Assuming the application design includes fault tolerance, setting up tests that mimic failure conditions helps ensure that applications keep running if a single scale unit fails, recover properly if all scale units go down, and do not corrupt or lose data under any circumstances.
- **Measure cost** Utility pricing models and the ability to automate on-demand resource provisioning, if not managed carefully, can lead to some surprising bills. Just as mobile phone users need to understand extra charges if they (or their children) exceed usage limits, enterprise IT teams should design tests to see how costs rise when large applications scale out in different scenarios.
- **Scale out** Testing to ensure that an application can scale out, even to levels higher than expected, can be a great long-term investment. Designing test scenarios for some multiple of the anticipated demand 5–10 years down the road can help you prevent higher development costs in the future. It is important to remember that although the cloud provides scale, you must ensure that your application has the ability to scale.
- **Simulate user access** For critical applications or those frequently used by field offices, simulate a user accessing the application from various on-premises and remote locations. Look for performance variability at different times of day. This will measure the overall performance of the solution, including the impact of network traffic and latency.
- **Isolate performance** Removing latency and network conditions from the picture can reveal how well the application itself performs. This requires that you run tests using a performance testing engine installed on a scale unit in the same cloud to isolate the application's performance from environmental factors such as Internet latency.

Operate in the Cloud

The largest concern enterprises often have about the cloud, after security, involves operations. Maintaining a hybrid ecosystem—as many enterprises will for the foreseeable future—does introduce complexity. Enterprises will proactively need to define an operational model that suits their needs, as cloud adoption inherently changes operational roles and responsibilities.

Support

Any good operational model starts with clearly defined roles, responsibilities, and accountabilities. Major cloud providers have tiered support models. It is important for enterprises to define clearly how, and under what conditions, internal IT staff will interact with cloud providers' support tools and personnel. A clear understanding of the data and level of detail required when reporting issues is necessary for smooth execution. Some cloud providers offer a technical account manager to oversee support and performance reviews, which is quite attractive for most enterprises.

Management

A cloud provider can either eliminate the need for certain tasks (such as software patching) or make them better, faster, or cheaper to manage (such as rolling data backups and snapshots). Before you undertake large-scale migrations, we recommend creating a manageability matrix to map enterprise and cloud provider roles and responsibilities against the operational services provided by on-premises teams. Keeping track of who is managing what for the enterprise will make it easier to investigate and resolve issues once applications are up and running in the cloud.

If you are using IaaS to host applications, IT operations staff still needs to manage operating systems and platforms. Some cloud providers, such as Amazon, maintain libraries of prebuilt images running different sets of operating systems and application platform stacks to make initial installation less time-consuming. Updates can certainly be automated to some degree as well.

While PaaS platforms perform rolling upgrades of the operating system, they of course do not manage upgrades to your IT applications. Shifting IT processes more toward a DevOps model, as described in Chapter 3, can make release management more efficient. In addition, operations can often perform rolling application upgrades to individual scale units. If designed properly, the applications can allow for upgrades without incurring downtime.

Monitoring

If they are freed from commodity tasks such as rolling out system updates to hundreds of physical servers, operations engineers can focus instead on measuring, monitoring, and improving applications and services. Having appropriate tools is crucial to this new charter. Some cloud providers support familiar on-premises tools, while others provide portals and APIs specific to their service offerings. In either case, it might be necessary to create custom tools.

It is possible for a service to appear available, based purely on the scale unit and web host status, but it is more accurate to monitor it based on the business definition of whether the service is healthy. You might think a service is fine, whether it is on-premises or in the cloud. In reality, however, users may not be able to complete their tasks. With the right definition, and with automated scripts that simulate transactions, operations personnel should know the application availability status that business users are experiencing at any given time—ideally uncovering issues *before* the first user reports a problem. Using the cloud frees up more time to ensure this is the case.

Most leading cloud providers offer visibility into core performance and availability metrics of their platform. They make the most vital and meaningful measurements available through portals, data feeds, or APIs. If they do not provide some information that interests enterprise CIOs, such as disk performance or I/O metrics, you can ask them for it or measure it yourself.

Many cloud providers also pull support-related feeds from data center monitoring systems. Other communication mechanisms can include wikis and blogs that keep customers informed of major maintenance or progress toward a resolution during an outage.

Today, monitoring in the cloud adds a bit of upfront work, but over time, we expect to see considerable improvement in the system health and monitoring tools that are available to cloud customers.

Business Continuity and Disaster Recovery

Moving services to highly available cloud infrastructures can improve business continuity. However, the redundancy built into such offerings is not enough to make cloud services disaster-proof. Human error can still wreak havoc. If data is triplicated on a cloud platform and an administrator inadvertently presses "Delete," that data is simply deleted in all three places.

Taking advantage of cloud services does not change the fact that BCDR involves a combination of business processes and technology tools. The advantage is that it provides more options. For example, cloud providers make tools available to their customers, along with a global reach that allows enterprises to protect against geo-specific disasters.

Data synchronization technologies, coupled with the ability to choose regions for deploying applications and databases, make it easy to implement BCDR for services. A critical application could deploy minimally scaled instances of the application and its data in an additional geographic region, thereby keeping it on standby. At the first sign of trouble, it could redirect users to these instances and scale up accordingly.

Measure Success

As with any initiative, having clear success metrics for your move to the cloud and measuring against them is vital. It is important that you take measurements regularly over the months or years it takes for an enterprise to complete its migration process to see whether any meaningful trends emerge. Most likely, it will be easier to quantify the cloud's contribution to cost savings than its direct contribution to revenues. We recommend tracking a number of variables.

Financial Impact

- Overall spending on IT
- Capital expenditures for hardware and software licenses
- Vendor costs (such as systems integrators, engineering resources, and consultants)
- Training costs
- Carbon footprint of the enterprise

Engineering Efficiency

- Total number of applications (assuming use of shared services built into the cloud)
- Number of person-hours used to create, support, and maintain applications
- Number of person-hours it takes to provision and manage data center hardware
- Reduction in development and testing person-hours achieved by using shared services, finished services, and so on
- Ratio of onsite administrators to applications
- Support tickets and costs (resulting from greater environment consistency and less support responsibilities)
- Size, number, and type of batch jobs processed during off-peak hours
- Idle server capacity (for example, overall resource utilization will increase)
- Operational expenditures, including staffing and cost of compute instances, data storage, and network usage
- Investment in tools for system administration, monitoring, and security

Agility

- Development cycle time
- Delays in application development resulting from capacity constraints
- Time it takes an IT service to reach production after the business requests it
- Time it takes to increase capacity
- Time to receive accurate data or perform analytics

Quality of Service

- Performance issues for applications in production resulting from capacity constraints
- Number of outages or significant performance issues
- Application response times, particularly for users located in distributed regions
- Network latency

Summary

- In the cloud, IT should focus on the entire set of IT systems to see where information, service, and process requirements converge to enable greater efficiencies, cost savings, and increased agility.
- Most enterprises will initially use hybrid architectures, for example, to keep data on-premises. Hybrid architectures require attention to latency and security issues that arise when connecting to the public Internet.
- Cloud-based applications live outside the corporate firewall and thus have a larger attack surface. Enterprises will need to re-examine their policies and standards, architectures, development practices, operations, and incident response protocols thoroughly when moving applications to the cloud.
- To take full advantage of on-demand scaling, application logic needs to be modular and loosely coupled rather than monolithic, as it is in some legacy applications, so that instances can function independently.
- Removing unnecessary dependencies, adding retry logic, using a persistent cache, and operating multiple scale units of a single application across a cloud provider's "availability zones" all help make cloud-based applications more stable.
- Taking advantage of parallelization in the cloud—for requesting, processing, or storing data, or for executing business logic—improves performance and availability.
- To reduce latency, use caching, reduce "chattiness" and/or payloads between components, and globally distribute and replicate content.

- Some cloud providers offer tools that simulate cloud compute, scaling, or storage services in a local environment. Engineers should still fully test and validate the application in the cloud to ensure that the solution works as expected.
- For identity management, some cloud providers offer both authentication and authorization services via a federation or claims identity provider.
- To connect on-premises services with those hosted in a cloud environment, use an IP connectivity layer or take advantage of middleware that your cloud provider offers.
- When testing solutions in the cloud, you should be sure to mimic failure, measure cost, scale out, simulate user access, and isolate an application's performance from environmental factors, such as Internet latency.
- Before undertaking large-scale migrations, create a manageability matrix to map enterprise and cloud provider roles and responsibilities against the operational services provided by on-premises teams.
- Monitor services based on whether users can complete their tasks, rather than relying on the server and web host status.
- Take measurements regularly to quantify performance and to discover whether meaningful trends emerge.

Epilogue

Emerging Markets and the Cloud

Throughout this book, we have asserted that moving to the cloud can help enterprises lower their total cost of ownership, increase return on business investments, and improve the speed at which innovative new products and services are brought to market.

One of the underlying assumptions of our guidance has been that you, like most CIOs and IT professionals, oversee a number of long-running legacy systems that may need reworking to operate optimally in the cloud. If your enterprise is typical, it also includes data center infrastructure that can be challenging and expensive to maintain.

This book's Prologue mentions the three activities of IT: sustain existing products and services, improve them, and introduce new ones—this is what Gartner calls "run, grow, and transform." The Gartner statistics cited state that in 2011, 66 percent of IT spending sustained existing products and services, 20 percent helped improve them, and 14 percent enabled the introduction of new products and services.[12]

Do you wish that you had the opportunity to invest a greater percentage of your IT spending in "transform" and "grow" activities instead of the 66 percent of IT spending that goes toward "running" activities today?

If you were *not* dealing with well-established legacy systems or data center infrastructure, would your IT strategy be different? What if you were a startup rather than an established company? What if you were based in an emerging market? What if you were a multinational in the midst of expanding your business into emerging markets where you did not yet have IT infrastructure or systems? What if you were looking to introduce an e-governance program in your city, state, or country?

[12]Source: Gartner, IT Metrics: Spending and Staffing Report, 2011, January 2011.

Whether you are a leader for a company in an emerging market or a leader for a multinational with expanding operations in emerging markets, cloud computing can provide game-changing opportunities.

Explosive Economic Growth

After spending the past 23 years in the United States, one of the authors of this book (Raj Biyani) recently relocated to India to lead Microsoft's IT operations in Hyderabad. As part of getting current on India, we studied India's economic history during the past two centuries and were stunned by what we discovered.

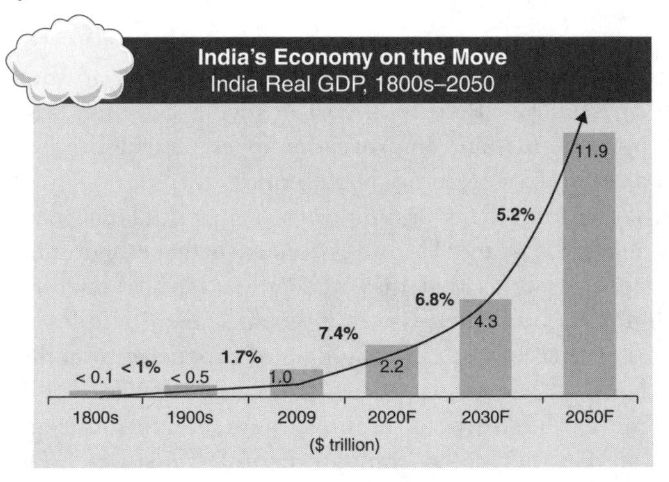

Since the 1800s, India's gross domestic product (GDP) has grown from a small base to over USD $1.5 trillion today and is projected to cross $2 trillion within the decade. To put this into context, India will experience more wealth creation during the next decade than it did during the previous two centuries!

This story is being played out in several emerging markets around the world. Microsoft's fastest growing market, for example, is Brazil. Whereas established markets may have reached saturation points and experience stiff competition that drives down margins, emerging markets promise many millions of potential new customers who are eager for the conveniences that wealthier countries take for granted.

Empirical evidence from around the world shows that for a country to achieve enough growth to transition from an emerging to a developed market, it needs infrastructure support. In addition to physical infrastructure (power, water, roads, bridges, airports, and so on), a robust IT infrastructure will be essential to experience this kind of growth.

So should emerging markets follow the conventional model of investing in traditional IT infrastructure, or can they skip a generation and go directly to IT in the cloud?

The Opportunity: Leapfrogging Legacy Technology

Many people in emerging markets have skipped technology trends, such as landline phones, which are still entrenched in mature markets. This "technology leapfrogging" allows those in emerging markets to adopt newer standards more quickly and in greater numbers. Even if a new technology offers less functionality than a mature market would expect, it will invariably be cheaper than more powerful alternatives, meeting the cost requirements of emerging markets, and it will offer more utility than the emerging market customer had before the technology was available. A path to success, then, is to offer products and services that are inexpensive as well as accessible from devices that might lack high-end features.

One such notable opportunity involves mobile phones. Even in areas that lack basic infrastructure such as roads and indoor plumbing, mobile phones are widely used. According to figures published in the Central Intelligence Agency publication, "The World Factbook,"[13] in India and China, one mobile phone subscriber exists for every two people. Brazil has even higher penetration with more than four mobile phones for every five people.

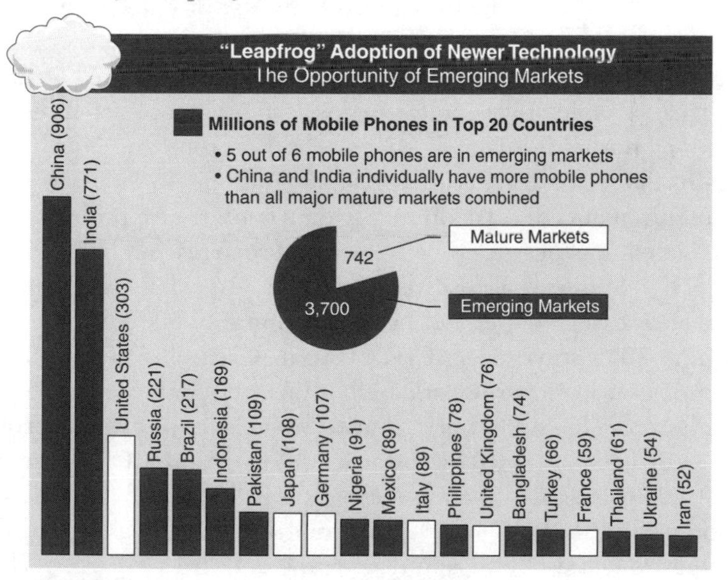

[13]https://www.cia.gov/library/publications/the-world-factbook/

Through mobile phones, companies can bring services to those who may not have access through any other means. For example, many Indians, even those who live in urban areas, may have to travel inconvenient distances to find a bank ATM (if they have a bank account at all), wait in long lines to pay bills, or pay 15 percent premiums to send cash to family members via couriers who might get robbed. If it were possible to connect to an online banking service in the cloud and transfer funds via mobile phone, many people would likely use such a service.

Another example is the proliferation of inexpensive PCs or thin clients. Cloud services, particularly Software as a Service (SaaS) offerings, do not necessarily require the fastest processors or the largest hard drives. People can opt for the most basic, even stripped-down hardware. They will still need Internet connectivity, but providers will continue to expand and enhance networks, as it is in their interests to serve more customers.

A core benefit of using the cloud to launch products and services in developing economies is faster time to market, which can translate into first-mover advantages. In countries that lack electricity, broadband support, and skilled labor, pooling resources via cloud providers is also an economical option.

IT does not yet have the foothold in developing countries that it has in developed countries. IT departments in developing countries can therefore "leapfrog" technology widely adopted elsewhere, just as consumers have done. The unrealized benefits for enterprises across all industries and the public sector are vast in these markets.

As economies grow, so, too, will their need and desire for the solutions IT can enable. Today, unfortunately, the type of custom enterprise applications hosted in many IT shops across Europe and North America are unaffordable or infeasible in developing nations. In India, for example, power requirements make maintaining data centers cost prohibitive for all but the largest businesses. Moving to cloud services can help reduce this barrier. The cloud can also serve companies, especially small and medium-size businesses, that do not have the capital to build data centers.

A June 2011 survey from GfK Custom Research confirms the adoption trend, showing a particularly high affinity to cloud services in emerging markets.[14] The study notes that a broad variety of cloud solutions have already been accepted by countries such as Brazil, China, and India. It also finds that issues such as data security, while often viewed as an adoption barrier to those in developed markets, is seen as among the key advantages to cloud offerings in developing countries.

---

[14]http://www.gfk.com/group/press_information/press_releases/008354/index.en.html

India: Platform Playground

India is a unique and powerful geography for platform vendors. This is due in part to India's end-to-end IT capabilities and offerings. Although many countries invest in IT, India not only invests in it as a customer, but the country is also home to many global IT players that build great software products or provide services to clients globally. This is important, because these players have an impact on the adoption success or failure of a given platform.

The cloud can be seen as a meta-platform, or a platform of platforms. Although Windows and Linux are "platforms" that can host line-of-business applications written in languages such as .NET and Java, the cloud hosts these operating systems themselves and provides additional value-add capabilities. History has shown that the success of any platform depends on a strategy that provides ecosystem players with what they need and want, whether directly or through partner relationships, and the one with the greatest number of tenants often wins.

Microsoft got this right at the dawn of the PC revolution, empowering ISVs and partners to develop easily on top of Windows and Office, enabling them to target a massive customer base. Apple is reemphasizing this phenomenon through the iPhone and iPad, with millions of applications being sold through its App Store. The cloud, in some sense, is no different, and which platforms India IT throws its weight behind will be an important factor given India's strong IT capabilities and the trend of outsourcing.

Although India, through its IT players, will have influence on the direction of cloud computing, there are other reasons why it is an important market to watch and participate in. These reasons include the following:

- **Untapped potential** India is not close to saturation levels in IT use and adoption. Unlike the Americas and Europe, Middle East and Africa (EMEA) regions, India and the Asia Pacific (APAC) regions have untapped IT potential at every level across the enterprise and public sector spaces. Combined with the leapfrogging phenomenon, this presents plenty of market growth potential. Are you taking advantage of India's IT growth potential?
- **Fertile resources** India is a ripe playground for piloting technology adoption, and many large Indian companies set up

Centers of Excellences largely for that purpose. India's combination of skilled IT developers and professionals, along with easy access to vendors and ISVs, make it a low-friction environment for experimenting with new trends. Is your organization taking advantage of India's resources?

- **Abundant opportunities** The small and midsized business (SMB) story in India is just warming up, and many in that community are starting to see some of India's largest problems as great opportunities. Even if you represent a large enterprise, ask yourself, how can I empower the multitude of smaller institutions through cloud services? A wealth of opportunity lies not just at the top, but also toward the base of the pyramid.

It is also important to note that factors such as data sovereignty regulations have helped lead to the rise of Indian domestic cloud offerings, which presents another potential opportunity. This is particularly true in sectors such as banking, financial services, insurance, healthcare, and the public sector.

Although regulation creates new domestic niches to fill, the overall attractiveness of cloud computing appeals greatly to small and large companies alike. India's technology giants—including Infosys, Reliance, Tata, and Wipro—all provide cloud services. Given the ample opportunities, it is no wonder India is often a great strategic investment and, if nothing else, a great playground for new technologies such as the cloud.

(Adapted with permission from the works of cloud computing expert and evangelist Janakiram MSV.)

Although emerging markets are poised for significant growth in cloud computing, it is important to note that this growth is not just a function of technology adoption but also the result of entrepreneurship and new innovations. For example, while India is poised for massive growth in SaaS offerings such as Microsoft Office 365, SalesForce's Force.com, and Google Docs, it is also home to Zoho, a competitive upstart with more than two dozen offerings ranging from collaboration to business and productivity applications. In this scenario, an emerging market entrant is competing globally with cloud offerings provided by companies based in developed markets.

Even the smallest of ventures, such as individual developers who make use of the cloud's low-cost tools and marketplaces, can now enter the market with relative ease. Anyone can submit an application to a mobile phone marketplace (sometimes for free); customers will not care where the service comes from as long as it works well and does something useful. There is no need for developers of phone applications to raise substantial funds, compete for limited shelf space in a physical store, or spearhead a marketing campaign. The cloud can level the playing field from California to Kenya for anyone with a good idea. This is particularly important, as there is an abundance of small businesses and entrepreneurs present in many emerging markets, oftentimes with an increased willingness to take risks relative to those in developed nations.

Case Studies

The following case studies highlight how the cloud, and in one instance a cloud-style solution, have brought great things to life and have had transformative results. Although the examples relate to India, many of the conclusions can be applied to other emerging markets across the globe.

Case Study: redBus.in, Riding the Cloud Bus

It was 2005 during the midst of India's greatest annual celebration, Diwali, known as the festival of lights. A young engineering graduate, back in his hometown to enjoy the occasion, is left temporarily stranded after an unsuccessful search for available bus tickets. Set back by a combination of notoriously bad traffic and seat sellouts, an idea emerges: Why not sell bus tickets over the Internet?

Fast forward to present day: redBus has sold more than 5.5 million bus tickets across India, working with hundreds of bus operators. Facing their own issues of scale four years after launching, redBus decided to move 100 percent into the cloud.

As is the case with many successful startups, predicting demand can be a challenge. Issues with their on-premises hosting, including downtime during peak booking hours, network configuration challenges, and a hardware upgrade cycle that took three weeks to complete, made it clear that their hosting model was not sustainable given the tremendous growth. Furthermore, the idea for a new business, an inventory management solution known as Bus Operator Software Services (BOSS), had just emerged. "We were skeptical on how successful adoption of this new business would be as the Indian bus industry is not known for its tech-savvy. It was important to minimize upfront investment," recalls Phanindra Sama, CEO of redBus.

The combination of factors made cloud computing the logical choice. Despite the fact that public cloud models were still in their relative infancy, in three short months, redBus had moved its entire business to the cloud. As expected, redBus was able to reduce costs, scale on demand, and implement a level of automation that allowed it to focus more on its core business. However, what was eye-opening was a near-instantaneous increase in sales of more than 25 percent. As redBus CTO Charan Padmaraju explains, "We were losing opportunities. Nothing else changed so there was no other explanation outside of the fact that we were losing sales due to lack of scalability."

The cloud also reduced the need for additional labor, resulting in added savings. While at one point redBus was contemplating hiring a database administrator, it was determined that the level of performance fine-tuning typically necessary on-premises would not be required due to cloud scaling and architectural paradigms. Coupled with this were the developer efficiencies gained by being able to destroy and re-create development and test environments at the click of a button, enabling developers to try new ideas otherwise not possible with the on-premises constraints.

The eventual success of BOSS transformed the company from a portal for consumers to buy tickets at their convenience to a SaaS provider digitizing bus operators. In the case of redBus, the cloud not only improved its existing business by providing the freedom to grow, reduce costs, and focus, but it also enabled the company to become a cloud solution provider.

Although scale challenges are what brought redBus to the cloud, the most important learning had to do with its impact to entrepreneurship and the ability to breed new businesses. As Sama concludes, "While the Internet era offers lower barriers to entry than that of the Industrial Revolution, cloud computing decreases those barriers even further. With the cloud entrepreneurs need not worry about infrastructure, and that fact alone is allowing so many more ideas, including some of ours, to see the light of day."

Case Study: Infosys, "Cloudvolution"

It's no secret that one of the fastest growing businesses in India is providing skilled technical resources to companies in other countries at an economical cost—a model known as "offshoring" or "outsourcing." Two key competitive areas for companies providing outsourced IT services are employee knowledge and speed of solution delivery.

Infosys pioneered the Global Delivery Model (GDM), which combines taking work to a geography with the best talent alongside minimizing costs and risks. This helped lead to the rise of offshoring in India, and the model now supports thousands of IT projects across a diverse set of industries that use a variety of computing platforms.

In an effort to bring further efficiency to GDM, Infosys saw an opportunity to use cloud computing to collaborate with customers more efficiently and respond to their needs more quickly, all while reducing costs. The aim of the initiative that followed, tagged "Cloudvolution," was to "conceptualize, design, and deploy" transformative cloud platforms that would change how business and IT services were delivered to its clients. As part of the initiative, five cloud platforms were defined; they are summarized in the following table (source: Infosys):

Platform	Description
MyCloud	A private cloud that powers the Infosys project delivery environment. It is used internally for both concept and software development activities.
IS Cloud	A private cloud that hosts Infosys IT applications used internally by the company.
Collaboration Cloud	An externally accessible cloud used to drive co-creation with external research bodies and academic institutions. It is also used as a platform for hosting labs, proofs-of-concept, and so on.
Cloud Ecosystem Integrator	A cloud environment used to help Infosys customers set up cloud platforms, and build and migrate applications to other clouds.
Business Platform Cloud	A cloud environment that services applications and solutions developed by various Infosys business units. These applications address various enterprise themes (such as Smarter Organization) and also cater to industry verticals such as banking and manufacturing.

Through Cloudvolution, Infosys was able to reduce costs significantly while providing benefits that improved the speed of project start time and, ultimately, solution delivery. For example, consolidating its infrastructure reduced hardware costs by 22 percent. It reduced hardware power consumption by 80 percent. According to Infosys internal analysis, it now takes six hours versus four to six weeks to set up a project environment.

Although several of today's environments run private clouds based on Windows Server Hyper-V, future plans might include integration with public cloud platforms, such as Windows Azure and Amazon Web Services, to increase agility and scale even further.

Case Study: India Department of Income Tax, e-Governance

The taxpayer base in India has grown significantly year over year, while the capacity of the Department of Income Tax (DIT) to process tax returns has remained constant. As a result, DIT fell further and further behind in issuing refunds and recovering underpayments. The government had to pay interest on delayed refunds, administrative costs increased, and taxpayers were unhappy.

To help alleviate these problems, DIT proposed creating a Centralized Processing Center (CPC) to handle all of India's electronically filed income tax returns. The goal was to update, automate, and standardize processes to make them more efficient, thereby increasing DIT's ability to manage the volume of returns they were receiving. The Indian government approved the proposal in February 2009 and established the CPC in Bangalore.

Award Winning e-Governance
CPC Provides a Full Set of Capabilities
Citations for e-Governance
Award
WINNERS
2011
EXCELLENCE IN GOVERNMENT PROCESS RE-ENGINEERING
GOLD AWARD
The following activities occur at the CPC:
• Receipt, scanning, and digitization of paper returns
• Acceptance and scanning of income tax return forms
• Tax payment accounting
• Processing of electronic and paper returns
• Delivery of intimations, demand notices, and issuance of refunds
• Processing requests for recertification
• Call center for queries, requests, and grievances from taxpayers
• Off-site storage of returns

Source: Government of India

According to Sanjai Kumar Verma, the commissioner of income tax who leads the CPC, the number of electronically filed tax returns grew to almost 10 million over two years and, as of this writing, was expected to hit the 20 million mark soon. In 2011, the CPC received the e-Governance Gold Award from the government of India.

The simplicity of the program and the availability of low-cost agencies to provide assistance made e-filing very attractive to taxpayers. The processing of e-filed returns has become much faster, which means taxpayers get their refunds sooner. As Verma said to the *Times of India* in July 2011, "Prior to the CPC, refunds used to take 15–18 months. Now it's just 89 days. People are eager to get their refunds quickly, and that's encouraging them to e-file." The goal now is to reduce cycle time to one month.[15]

The CPC took a novel approach to provisioning the system infrastructure by forming a public/private partnership with a solution provider. The provider installed the IT systems and was paid on a per-transaction model not unlike the utility pricing cloud providers offer. This way, the CPC avoided problems with proper sizing of resources.

Case Study: Microsoft, Windows Azure Sandbox

To build internal momentum for cloud adoption, Microsoft IT decided to launch the Windows Azure Sandbox. Through the Sandbox, Microsoft IT centrally funds subscriptions to Windows Azure and SQL Azure for Microsoft employees and interns, at the low cost of a few dollars a month per participant. Microsoft IT India, where 80 percent of employees have been trained on Windows Azure, has been particularly enthusiastic about the Sandbox.

Implementing the Sandbox Microsoft IT nests as many as 500 subscriptions within each Azure account, making subscriptions available to individual developers who are registered as "service administrators." Developers can experiment with the technology however they want, but since Microsoft IT owns the accounts, it can take control of a subscription at any point.

As part of managing the program, Microsoft IT introduced an automated tracking and reporting mechanism, which sends each user a weekly e-mail summarizing his or her resource usage. The e-mail alerts users who are going over their quota and gives them instructions for how to reduce their resource consumption.

The Windows Azure Sandbox administrator controls the rate of new subscriptions to ensure that participation growth stays in line with the

[15]"E-filing of Income Tax returns sees a spurt." *Times of India.* http://articles.timesofindia.indiatimes.com/2011-07-26/india-business/29815673_1_e-filing-returns-income-tax

program's monthly spending targets. Microsoft IT has been able to demonstrate a predictable spending model to its finance counterparts. "We are not seeing massive spikes in use one month with nothing the following month," says Matt Hempey, a Microsoft IT Director who started the Windows Azure Sandbox. "It's been very steady and consistent. It's a great example of how asking employees to manage their own use of company resources can be more flexible and efficient than in a centralized model. It's a management system that works."[16]

Lowering Barriers Getting access to cloud-based resources via the Sandbox is easy. Approval for a subscription takes less than 24 hours. Developers who need more compute cycles, storage, or services than a basic Sandbox account offers can apply for a second-tier subscription that provides more resources. Sandbox users do not have to submit a business justification for building an application, nor do they need to get executive approval, ask for funding, or stick to a schedule. Instead, they can build a proof-of-concept or prototype application on Windows Azure in their spare time, with no out-of-pocket costs. Co-workers from around the world can experiment with their prototypes and provide feedback.

Fostering a Community The Sandbox taps into an internal development community known as The Garage to encourage grassroots innovation. The community serves as an open forum for vetting ideas and asking questions through e-mail or in person. It is a venue for sharing discoveries and techniques on new technologies that could feed into architectural planning for IT applications.

To nurture a vibrant community, The Garage has gone beyond establishing e-mail distribution lists, putting up internal websites, and handing out branded T-shirts. It also sponsors contests and gives employees a chance to showcase their ideas through The Garage Science Fairs, which it hosts regularly in Redmond, Washington, and in Hyderabad, India, attracting hundreds of employees from all around the company.

Microsoft also sponsors virtual challenges, such as one that gave cash awards to the most innovative prototypes developed using both Windows Phone and Azure platforms. Garage awards not only create incentive to participate, but also result in greater visibility and credibility to concepts generated within the community.

Enabling Innovation The Sandbox reached 4000 Microsoft employees within 14 months (as shown in the following illustration) and is still going strong. Participants have created innovative solutions ranging

[16]"Sandbox Accelerates Grassroots Innovation in Windows Azure Development." Microsoft IT Showcase. http://www.microsoft.com/download/en/details.aspx?id=26206

from a Green IT prototype envisioned in India that tracks computer energy consumption, to sample applications that demonstrate the power of the cloud to independent software vendors in Serbia.

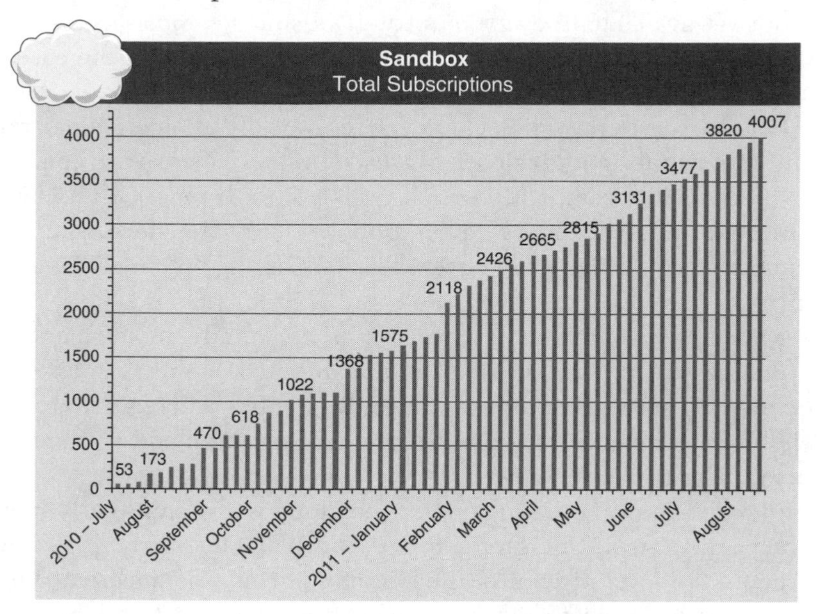

Sandbox projects are also helping development teams innovate in the cloud faster. Some teams, such as Microsoft Office, have used the Sandbox to investigate Windows Azure before making a decision to invest fully in using the platform for their services.

The Windows Azure Sandbox is not only helping Microsoft IT train employees in cloud technologies, it is also encouraging a culture of enthusiastic grassroots innovation.

As Hempey puts it, "We see a lot of informal participation across the company. I would say the percentage is much higher in India. Why that's the case, I wouldn't venture a guess, but I would say that the spirit of innovation is very alive in Hyderabad.... This is the place where there is an unusual degree of enthusiasm for doing things at the grass-roots level."[17]

Emerging Market Challenges

Along with opportunities, adopting cloud computing in emerging markets also comes with challenges. Governments that see the potential of the cloud to help their economies grow are making large investments.

[17] "Good ideas can come from anywhere." Livemint.com, HT Media. http://www.livemint.com/2011/07/12230803/Matt-Hempey—Good-ideas-can-c.html?h=B

China, for example, is building a city-sized data center complex that will be the largest in Asia.

Cloud computing is still relatively young, however, and local services are not yet available in every country. If businesses must access cloud services located in a different country, latency issues can increase, as may risks associated with storing data in a foreign location.

One barrier to providing cloud services locally in emerging markets is Internet connectivity, which is inconsistent and expensive in countries that lack provider competition. Another is power. If power is unreliable, then cloud data centers, whether public or private, need their own backup systems, which add to overall costs. Getting potential customers to trust in the overall reliability of a cloud service, including its ability to meet SLAs, is also an important factor, as it would be in any market.

Businesses, particularly small and medium-sized ones, can also have incentives to keep operations in-house. In markets where software piracy is high, companies may fear that leveraging the cloud will increase costs rather than lower them.

In many countries, regulation of the cloud is also in its early stages. Privacy and security are often a mixed bag, as is the ability to give governments the level of control they demand. This was apparent during Google's struggles with the Chinese government and with the pressures that India and the Middle East put on Research in Motion regarding the BlackBerry's use of encryption.

It goes without saying that any cloud provider you select for an emerging market must understand the local culture and business climate, including local laws. In addition, it should demonstrate a long-term commitment to that market, for example, through partnerships with universities or telecom providers. The features and pricing it offers should also be appropriate for the country's stage of economic development.

Summary

- If you are a leader in a company in an emerging market or a multinational that plans to expand into an emerging market, the cloud offers unprecedented opportunity.
- Create a cloud strategy for emerging markets early in your planning process, in case the business asks for your help bringing a product or service to an emerging market quickly.
- Many emerging markets have skipped technology trends, leaving them free to adopt newer standards more quickly and in greater numbers.

Products and services that are inexpensive and accessible from lower-end devices will succeed more easily.

- The main benefit of using the cloud to launch products and services in developing economies is faster time to market, which can translate into first-mover advantages.
- In countries that lack electricity, broadband support, and skilled labor, pooling resources via cloud providers creates economic benefits.
- Barriers to cloud computing in emerging markets include lack of Internet connectivity, power, and regulations. Select cloud providers that understand the local culture and business climate, including local laws, and demonstrate a long-term commitment to that market.

Glossary

Active Directory Federation Services (ADFS) A standards-based service that allows the secure sharing of identity information among trusted business partners (known as a federation) across networks. When a user needs to access a web application from one of its federation partners, the user's own organization is responsible for authenticating the user and providing identity information in the form of "claims" to the partner that hosts the web application. The hosting partner uses its trust policy to map the incoming claims to claims that are understood by its web application, which uses the claims to make authorization decisions.[18]

addressable spend The portion of the IT budget that moving to the cloud can impact to reduce cost.

administrative tooling Tools that help with the administration of cloud services.

Amazon Relational Database Service (Amazon RDS) A web service that makes it easy to set up, operate, and scale a relational database in the cloud.[19]

Amazon Web Services (AWS) A set of services that together form a reliable, scalable, and inexpensive computing platform "in the cloud."[20]

application programming interface (API) A set of rules used for communicating across components of an application.

application segmentation The process of sorting applications into Basic, Intermediate, and Advanced categories based on business and technical criteria.

---

[18]"Active Directory Federation Services." Microsoft MSDN. http://msdn.microsoft.com/en-us/library/bb897402.aspx

[19]"Amazon Relational Database Service (Amazon RDS)" http://aws.amazon.com/rds/

[20]"Amazon Web Services." http://aws.amazon.com/

binary large objects (BLOBs) Images, videos, data, or documents stored as flat files instead of in a tabular format. BLOB storage services provide some structure, such as folders.

Business Process as a Service (BPaaS) An offering that provides part or all of a business process, as opposed to a single application. A BPaaS might even knit together services from multiple vendors.

capital expenditure (CAPEX) Expenses for fixed assets that generally have a useful life of more than one year.

content delivery network (CDN) A set of geographically distributed connected nodes where data is replicated and stored to reduce latency when the data is accessed.

cloud bursting The ability to spill over on-premises workloads to cloud environments.

cloud platform The cloud software and infrastructure that provides the computing, storage, and management services for hosting applications and services.

cloud service An IT solution that is delivered and consumed over the Internet or an intranet hosted on a cloud platform. Services range from e-mail to entire IT platforms.

community cloud A cloud infrastructure shared by a group of organizations with common goals or concerns, such as civil agencies. It can be managed by the group or by a third party and can be hosted on-premises or off-premises.

Data as a Service (DaaS) Through web services and standards such as Open Data Protocol (OData), DaaS provides access to data, such as census statistics, that applications can mine, analyze, visualize, and so on. The provider manages the data and its quality, while customers have on-demand access to the data at scale, generally for a reasonable price.

elasticity The ability to increase or reduce storage, network bandwidth, or compute capacity almost immediately, allowing customers to scale their solution for optimal resource usage.

EXT3 A common file system used by Linux-based distributions (operating systems).

fabric controller Software in the cloud that provisions resources, balances loads, manages servers, performs operating system updates, and ensures that environments are available.

The Health Insurance Portability and Accountability Act of 1996 (HIPAA) United States standards for the security of electronic protected health information, including confidentiality provisions of the Patient Safety Rule, which protect identifiable information from being used to analyze patient safety events and improve patient safety.[21]

hybrid cloud A cloud infrastructure comprising two or more clouds (private, community, or public) that remain unique entities but are linked by technology that enables data and application portability (as defined by National Institute of Standards and Technology).

hybrid environment The integration of on-premises and cloud services that work together to serve a set of users or scenarios.

Infrastructure as a Service (IaaS) Cloud offerings that give customers the ability to run client/server applications on virtual machines (VMs). The vendor manages the network, servers, and storage resources, while the customer must still manage operating systems, the back-end stack, and applications.

ISO/IEC 27001:2005 The requirements for establishing, implementing, operating, monitoring, reviewing, maintaining, and improving a documented information security management system within the context of the organization's overall business risks. The standard specifies requirements for the implementation of security controls customized to the needs of individual organizations or parts thereof.[22]

JavaScript Object Notation (JSON) A lightweight data-interchange format based on a subset of the JavaScript programming language. JSON is a text format that is completely language independent but uses conventions that are familiar to programmers of the C-family of languages.[23]

Microsoft Dynamics CRM Online A web-based customer relationship management service, available by subscription, used to manage sales, marketing, and IT support interactions. It works with the customer's deployment of Microsoft Outlook and can be customized to meet many relationship-management needs.

Microsoft Office 365 A component of Microsoft Online Services that delivers productivity solutions to businesses of all sizes. Office 365

[21]"Health Information Privacy." http://www.hhs.gov/ocr/privacy/
[22]"ISO/IEC 27001:2005." International Organization for Standardization. http://www.iso.org/iso/iso_catalogue/catalogue_tc/catalogue_detail.htm?csnumber=42103
[23]"Introducing JSON." http://www.json.org/

combines Microsoft Office Professional Plus desktop applications with Microsoft Exchange Online, SharePoint Online, and Lync Online.

Microsoft SharePoint A collaboration tool created by Microsoft used for content/document management and information sharing via a web platform.

Microsoft Visual Studio Microsoft's Integrated Development Environment (IDE) that provides a platform for application development for managed (such as C#, VB.NET) and unmanaged (such as C++) code.

monolithic software design Application design in which functionality, such as the user interface and business logic layers, is tightly integrated into one application component.

multitenancy Pooled hosting environments in which more than one organization's applications and data are hosted on the same infrastructure (for example, within the same server).

National Institute of Standards and Technology (NIST) The official U.S. technology agency that works with industry to develop and apply technology, measurements, and standards.[24]

off-premises A location that houses resources, such as servers, outside of the premises owned and operated by a company. Often called a third-party data center.

on-premises A location that houses resources, such as servers, in a location owned and operated by the company. This often refers to a corporate data center.

Open Data Protocol (OData) A web protocol and standard built on HTTP, Atom Publishing Protocol, and JSON to provide access to data from various sources, such as applications, databases, services, and stores. The aim of OData is to make it easier to integrate and share data from different sources.

operational expenditures (OPEX) Variable costs incurred during the course of running services, such as IT services, which are not fixed-asset capital expenditures. They include items such as personnel and maintenance costs.

---

[24]National Institute of Standards and Technology. http://www.nist.gov

parallelization A computational principle whereby more than one transaction is processed simultaneously.

Payment Card Industry (PCI) Data Security Standard Controls for information security created by the Payment Card Industry Security Standards Council that companies should follow when handling credit card information.

Platform as a Service (PaaS) A service delivery model used to develop, deploy, monitor, and maintain applications while the cloud provider manages everything else, including the operating system and middleware.

private cloud A cloud infrastructure that serves one organization while providing most core cloud benefits, whether the organization or a third party manages it on-premises or off-premises. This is the model of choice for enterprises with strong concerns about data security and information privacy.

provisioning The process by which resources (such as hardware and software) are made available for use.

public cloud A multitenant environment with massive global scale, resource-intensive capabilities such as content delivery networks, and cost savings through economies of scale. Customers will never need to provision, manage, upgrade, or replace hardware in a public cloud, as they would need to do with some private clouds.

real-time enterprise An enterprise that requires faster application development, a constant stream of data, and responsiveness that are not achievable with long-cycle planning and refreshes.

replicate, replication The process of distributing the same piece of data to multiple endpoints. Replication is often used for redundancy, disaster recovery, failover, or accessibility.

sandbox An environment for development that provides a place to test and validate new applications or pieces of code with minimal risk to critical production environments.

The Sarbanes-Oxley Act of 2002 (SOX) A U.S. federal law focused on financial and accounting compliance standards applicable to publicly held corporations. It has implications for IT systems and processes that hold data used in SOX audits and compliance reporting.

scalability The ability to change the available capacity of a system. Scaling can occur in three ways: scale up (also known as vertical scaling), increasing the available resources allocated to a scale unit, such as the amount of CPU and memory available for a VM or hardware on a server; scale out (also known as horizontal scaling), adding additional scale units for use by an application or service; and scale down, reducing the available capacity by reducing resources.

Secure Sockets Layer (SSL) A cryptographic protocol that encrypts network connections and is widely used for web browsing (such as HTTPS) and other forms of Internet traffic.

Security Development Lifecycle (SDL) A software development security assurance process that consists of a collection of security practices, grouped by the phases of the traditional software development lifecycle. The SDL process is not specific to Microsoft or the Windows platform. It can be applied to different operating systems, platforms, development methodologies, and projects.[25]

service bus A middleware platform that allows traffic to pass through enterprise firewalls via a publicly accessible endpoint. These services provide additional capabilities, such as multicast messaging, workflow, and durable storage. Messaging capabilities can allow integration between partners without requiring integration at the IP level

shadow IT applications IT applications built and managed outside of standard IT processes and often without approval of the central IT department.

shared services Centralized services used by multiple applications and multiple groups within a company.

Software as a Service (SaaS) A service delivery model in which companies subscribe to prepackaged applications that run on a cloud infrastructure and allow access from a variety of devices. Enterprises are rarely responsible for operations beyond some configuration and data quality management.

SQL Azure A relational database service based on SQL server technologies delivered in the cloud.

Statement of Auditing Standards No. 70 (SAS 70 Type I and II) Guidance created by the American Institute of Certified Public

[25]"Microsoft Security Development Lifecycle Process." Microsoft. http://www.microsoft.com/security/sdl/discover/default.aspx

Accountants for auditors of financial statements and internal controls. Type I refers to the auditor's report detailing the design and sustainability of the internal controls. Type II refers to the auditor's opinion on whether the controls were operating correctly during the audit period.

static content Content that does not change very often.

synthetic transactions Automated tests that simulate user transactions on a system (such as logging in, performing a query, or submitting a request), often used to test the performance and availability from a real-world perspective.

tablet A portable personal computer for which the primary user interface is a touch screen.

three-9s A shorthand way of describing 99.9 percent uptime availability of IT systems.

turnkey solution A finished service or product that the customer does not need to modify before first use.

Twitterverse A blend of the words "Twitter" and "universe" used in popular media to describe the community of Twitter users. Twitter is a social media service that allows users to publish and view short message posts on the Internet, to which others can subscribe.

user acceptance testing (UAT) A systematic validation methodology for an application or service to ensure the original requirements were met, whereby end users or service owners perform testing, generally of real-world scenarios and use cases, before the solution is released.

user interface (UI) layer The interface through which a user and application interact; the UI layer presents data and provides a way for a user to input data. It is often segmented from business logic and data storage layers.

virtual machine (VM) An operating system running in an isolated environment (guest) within a server operating system (host) that is using virtualization technologies. Virtual machines are akin to "virtual computers" running inside a server, allowing physical resources to be shared and multiple virtual environments to run in parallel inside a computer.

waterfall-style methodologies A model of software design engineering in which steps of the project are completed sequentially in a downward, or waterfall, pattern. Common phases of a waterfall-style project include requirements, design, implementation, and verification.

web proxy server A server that sits between end users and Internet web servers that can perform multiple functions such as retrieving data from websites on behalf of users, caching content, and website filtering based on rules.

web server A server running software that hosts content for users, such as websites, over a network.

Index

E

F

G

Q

R

S

U

V

W

Z

About the Authors

Pankaj Arora is a Senior Manager in the Microsoft IT Global Strategic Initiatives team. A thought leader on cloud computing, he has been integral in developing the enterprise business case for Microsoft IT, defining the internal cloud adoption strategy, and partnering with the Windows Azure team on platform readiness and competitive analysis. Pankaj was the technical lead for the first migration of a Microsoft IT application to Azure, and he also launched an initiative to move critical assets to the cloud. Prior to that, he managed a variety of high-impact IT systems, including the Microsoft Career Site.

Pankaj is a graduate of General Electric's Information Management Leadership Program and is certified in Six Sigma. He is also an entrepreneur, having launched a successful IT consulting company at a young age, for which he was featured in publications such as *Kiplinger's Personal Finance*. Pankaj holds a business degree with distinction from the University of Minnesota. He resides in Kirkland, Washington.

Raj Biyani is the Managing Director for Microsoft IT (India) and the Global Strategic Initiatives organization. Microsoft IT (India) is Microsoft's largest IT operation outside of corporate headquarters in Redmond, Washington.

Raj has demonstrated an ability to see opportunities early and generate executive support for initiatives to capitalize on those opportunities. Prior to joining Microsoft IT, Raj led the envisioning and successful creation of the Windows Marketplace, an electronic software delivery platform for Microsoft.

Raj holds a bachelor's degree in Computer Science and Accounting from Goshen College, Indiana, and an MBA with honors from the University of Chicago. He holds multiple EU and U.S. patents.

Raj has recently relocated from Bellevue, Washington, to Hyderabad, India, with his wife, Aarti, and their two young children, Garima and Rohan.

Salil Dave is a Senior Director in the Microsoft IT Global Strategic Initiatives team. In his 25-year career he has covered a range of industries and roles, including a decade at Microsoft, 6 years at supply chain software pioneer i2 Technologies, and 5 years at the Indian Revenue Service.

As an early member of i2's Strategic Services Group, Salil helped develop the Supply Chain Opportunity Assessment methodology, enabling informed and focused technology adoption in enterprises. At the Indian Revenue Service, Salil created the earliest systems for online processing of international trade transactions.

He has a BTech from the Indian Institute of Technology Kanpur, an MBA from the Indian Institute of Management Ahmedabad, and an MPA from Harvard University. He resides in Medina, Washington, with his wife, Rashmi, and sons, Ankur and Arjun.

BAKER COLLEGE LIBRARY
3 3504 00567 7606